Bush to Buckingham Palace

Crazy adventures of fun-loving test cricketer

Rick Darling

RYAN
PUBLISHING

First published 2022 by Ryan Publishing

PO Box 7680, Melbourne, 3004
Victoria, Australia
Ph: 61 3 9505 6820
Email: books@ryanpub.com
Website: www.ryanpub.com

**RYAN
PUBLISHING**

 A catalogue record for this
book is available from the
National Library of Australia

Title: *Bush to Buckingham Palace: Crazy adventures of
fun-loving test cricketer Rick Darling*

Paperback: 9781876498986
eBook: 9781876498993

Internal and cover design by Luke Harris, Working Type
Studio, Victoria, Australia. www.workingtype.com.au
Edited by Graeme Ryan
Illustrations by Tavis O'Hazy Robertson

Back cover image: Rick Darling and Kim Hughes enter the
Australian rooms at lunch on the second day of the Fourth
Test against England at the SCG on 7 January 1979.

After lunch, Rick went on to make his best Test score of 91
and was top scorer for Australia.

He featured in a partnership of 125 with Hughes followed by
one of 52 with his captain, Graham Yallop.

Words of Wisdom

"You probably won't remember the games you have played, if you win or lose, if you have performed or not, but what you will remember are the good times and camaraderie with your mates."
Bob Simpson, Australian Cricket Captain,
Barbados, 1978.

"And now that time advances
And evening shadows fall
Persuasion from the family
To summarise it all.
'Just write it down,' in chorus,
They say around the table,
'Preserve these stories for us,
While with us fit and able.'"

Arch Grosvenor 1983

Acknowledgements

This book is dedicated to my wife, Tania, and our children, Shannon, Zoe and Sam. Their interest and insistence prompted me to put on paper some of the stories that I had shared with them.

Trevor Gill for his expertise as an author and in journalism for the Introduction. His generosity, editing, mentoring and encouragement have been pivotal in the creation of this book. The assistance I sought from him has equated to many months of enjoyable learning for me.

Graeme Wood for writing the Foreword. He knew me better than anyone during my playing days. His words are appreciated.

Tavis O'Hazy Robertson for the skilful, comical sketches that he has produced.

Many other acquaintances have jolted my memory which have led to the writing of many of these reminiscences.

I have tried to present the stories in a chronological, factual manner, and apologise for any errors and omissions.

Rick Darling, Adelaide, 2022.

Rick's Test Batting Statistics

Span	Mat	Runs	HS	Bat Av
1978-1979	14	697	91	26.80

MATCH BY MATCH LIST

Bat1	Bat2	Runs	Ct	Opposition	Ground	Start Date
65	56	121	0	India	Adelaide	28 Jan 1978
4	8	12	1	West Indies	Bridgetown	17 Mar 1978
15	0	15	0	West Indies	Georgetown	31 Mar 1978
10	6	16	0	West Indies	Port of Spain	15 Apr 1978
25	5	30	0	England	Perth	15 Dec 1978
33	21	54	2	England	Melbourne	29 Dec 1978
91	13	104	1	England	Sydney	6 Jan 1979
15	18	33	1	England	Adelaide	27 Jan 1979
75	79	154	0	Pakistan	Perth	24 Mar 1979
7	DNB	7	0	India	Bengaluru	19 Sep 1979
59	4	63	0	India	Kanpur	2 Oct 1979
19	7	26	0	India	Delhi	13 Oct 1979
39	7	46	0	India	Kolkata	26 Oct 1979
16	0*	16	0	India	Wankhede	3 Nov 1979

Contents

Foreword

Graeme Wood

To be asked to contribute to someone's book and more importantly to write the Foreword of a book of a fellow Test cricketer, teammate and great friend is a real honour.

Warrick Maxwell Darling, the boy from Waikerie, a rural town in the Riverland region of South Australia with a current population of around 2,650, came from a tremendous cricket heritage with 'great uncle' Joe Darling and Prince Alfred College, where the Chappell brothers were educated.

I first met Rick two days prior to the fifth and deciding Test match against India in Adelaide in January 1978. We had both been selected to make our Test debuts, Rick aged 20 and myself aged 21, we had a brief introduction in the nets and told we would be opening the innings together. We were both very excited about the prospect and couldn't wait for the Test to commence.

Australia won the toss, and we were going to bat on

day one. I was ready, sitting, trying to relax as much as I could when suddenly Rick disappeared into the toilets, vomiting profusely due to his nervous state. Fortunately, he recovered and out we went, I'll never forget the walk down through the members area onto the Adelaide Oval, we shared an 89-run partnership, and we won the Test and the series. I immediately knew I had met and played with a mate I would have for the remainder of my cricket career and life in general.

Following the Adelaide Test, we toured the West Indies where we roomed together for the whole three months and became very close, both having similar interests and very much similar senses of humour. We played together in eight Test matches, numerous One Day Internationals and roomed together on an arduous tour of India in 1979. I'm sure this book will feature some of the experiences from both overseas tours.

Rick was an extremely talented cricketer, loved to hook and cut the quick bowlers, would have been a sensation if playing all his cricket at the WACA Ground, and was a tremendous player of spin bowling. He was recognised as one of the best cover fielders in world cricket, but as I alluded to, he was acutely nervous and had the misfortune of suffering several serious injuries very early in his international career. I'm sure if he had the support mechanisms available in world cricket today, would have played far more cricket for Australia.

Our first tour to the West Indies had 16 players and one manager, no other support staff, no coach, no doctor, no physio, etc. I saw a recent photograph of the Indian team touring the UK for the ICC Test Championship, they had 17 players and 20 support staff!

There is no doubt Warrick Maxwell Darling was one of the most popular players of his time for South Australia and Australia, with both his teammates and opposition players. He was an absolute pleasure to be around, and I'm sure everyone will enjoy this read and the explanation of the lighter side of his life and his life in cricket.

Thanks for the memories, mate.

Introduction

Trevor Gill, Adelaide. 2021.

As a young journalist with *The News* in Adelaide, one of my clear memories was being dispatched to the Riverland settlement of Ramco to interview Rick Darling. Rick had just been selected for his Sheffield Shield debut with the South Australian team and his rise to first-class cricket was an enticing story about a boy from the bush playing his way towards the pinnacle of his sport.

The shy 18-year-old who photographer Dennis Rogers and I met at Ramco was at first a little reluctant about stepping into the media spotlight having only recently graduated from playing for Waikerie to district cricket with Salisbury.

The idea of a picture batting in front of an upturned grape tin for a wicket with a few mates in the slips was enough to make him feel comfortable. Well, he wasted no time belting a few balls into the orchard at square leg!

On that same day in Ramco, Rick's mother, Lyla,

recalled, "When he was born the doctor phoned my husband and didn't tell him he had a son. He just said there was a new cricketer in the family." Rick's dad, Max, responded, "I gave that kid a bloody cricket bat when he was two years old, and I used to throw ping pong balls at him. I couldn't get him out then, and I'm damned if I can now!"

Rick admitted to a little case of nerves about his debut for South Australia against Queensland at Adelaide Oval in November 1975. Although he did not make a lot of runs in that match, it was memorable because his baptism at the crease was a missile attack from Jeff Thompson, arguably the world's fastest bowler. It was the beginning of a sporting journey that took Rick to the Australian team as an opening batsman and brilliant cover fieldsman, but also to a series of life-threatening cricket injuries that prematurely ended his Test career at 23 years of age.

Just as we had predicted on that dusty pitch by a meander of the Murray River five years earlier, Rick's rise to an outstanding career in first class cricket and in a sadly limited number of Test matches became a remarkable story of heroism under fire.

Almost five decades after we first met, Rick has not changed much from his laconic days in Riverland cricket playing with his knockabout mates answering to curious names like Alley Cat, Guts, Bucky, Punk, Crumby, Bub and Lordy. Having survived the toughest school of hard knocks, he has some wonderful memories of great characters and events in the game at all levels.

This book is a collection of some of those memories, some happy and others sad, yet all-defining about the make-up of Warrick Maxwell Darling with insights into the pressures and joys of playing the game of cricket.

As an introduction to Rick's souvenir thoughts and impressions, the following briefly outlines his career. It features excerpts from an article I wrote about Rick that appeared among other player profiles in the SACA's 150th anniversary Yearbook in 2021.

In his first year as a teenager, Rick Darling was playing cricket against men in a 'sink or swim' sporting environment that drove his destiny towards the pinnacle of the sport. He'd just turned 13, a schoolboy from a fruit block in the Riverland, when he first strode nervously to the crease at senior level for Waikerie.

"I remember playing against Blanchetown and opening the batting for Waikerie," Rick recalled. "I was dropped on nought, yet went on to make a century. That was the game changer for me. I had a lot of other sporting interests, and if I'd made a duck I may not have continued in cricket. Having scored a ton, I just wanted more."

Rick's batting prowess was honed on hard wickets with countless hours of practice under the direction of his dad, Max, an accomplished country all-rounder, and his two close cousins, Wayne, and Don Darling, both of whom played A-grade district cricket. The concrete pitches encouraged Rick to specialise in the hook shot, a weapon that hard-wired him to multitudes of runs, but also one that in the end literally knocked him out of the game.

From Waikerie, he played with distinction in the Shell Shield Under-16 competition in Adelaide and was enticed to Salisbury Cricket Club by Ernie Clifton, the former English first class cricketer and SACA coach. He made his A-grade debut for Salisbury at the age of 15 and some outstanding batting performances in the SACA Colts team put him on the radar for the Sheffield Shield side, making his first-class debut in South Australia's triumphant 1975-1976 season.

"Suddenly I was in the nets with blokes like Ian Chappell, Terry Jenner, Ashley Mallett and Ashley Woodcock," Rick said. "I was still pretty much a meek and mild country kid, always homesick, and it was a daunting prospect to be playing alongside such stars of the game. Yet I was embraced into the team atmosphere, and I was a good listener. I literally fed off the experience of those older fellows. Ian especially was very supportive, even though I had replaced his brother Trevor in the State team."

Rick's first Sheffield Shield game was in fact the first one he'd seen, and his introduction was a Queensland attack that featured Test pace pair Jeff Thomson and Geoff Dymock. "Thommo tried to york me first ball, but

I kept it out and got off the mark to go on and make five before being run out," he recalled. "It was not a noteworthy innings, but one thing I do remember about that game is that the SACA put me up at the Tea Tree Gully hotel and I had to catch the bus wearing T-shirt, thongs and footy shorts into Adelaide with my cricket bag to play."

Another young bloke in his debut season for South Australia in 1975-1976 was David Hookes, and the pair became dominating forces in the State side. "We were great mates until he tragically died in 2004," Rick said. "We looked up to Chappelli, although I always called him Ian. He was like a God to us. Ian had fashioned his aggressive approach to the game on his predecessor Les Favell, and Hookesy moulded himself on Chappelli. It was an era of great captaincy."

The seismic upheaval caused by World Series Cricket in 1976 and the defection of the biggest names in the game to Kerry Packer's rival competition shook the establishment to its core with the Australian Cricket Board scrambling to assemble a team to compete in the traditional format. Rick was still establishing his foothold in the South Australian team, but some excellent batting performances over several summers attracted the Australian selectors to the swashbuckling young batsman.

"All I wanted to do was play to the best of my ability," he said. "It was an awesome feeling to get a call up to the Australian team to play in the fifth Test against

India at Adelaide Oval in January 1978. I was out water skiing when the news came through and I had to rush to Adelaide."

Rick was 20 and his fellow opener, Graeme Wood, also making his Test debut, was 21. The two rookies with the world at their feet met for the first time two days prior to the match, and they went on to become the best of friends.

Rick performed admirably scoring 65 and 56 to secure a berth with Wood on the Australian tour of the West Indies in 1978 led by the veteran skipper Bob Simpson, who had been enticed out of retirement to steady the ship in the wake of the WSC rebellion.

While scoring well in some of the minor games in the 'Windies' against Trinidad and Tobago, Barbados, Guyana, and Bermuda counties it was a forgettable, injury-racked tour for Rick at Test level. Yet, back home, he was recalled to the Australian team to partner Graeme Wood in the fourth Ashes Test against England in Sydney on 6 January 1979.

In a powerful comeback, Rick top scored with 91 runs in the first innings, but England shattered the Australian second innings to win the Test by 93 runs.

Committed to hooking rather than ducking, Rick was a constant magnet for bouncers – a perilous pursuit against the best bowlers in the world. One vicious, rising, in-swinging delivery from English fast bowler Bob Willis in the fifth Test in Adelaide in February 1979 could have cost him his life. Hit above the heart, Rick collapsed on the pitch with chewing gum lodged in his throat. One of the English fielders rushed to his aid and thumped him on the chest, dislodging the chewy.

Reflecting on those dramatic moments, Rick said, "I'd also swallowed my tongue. Umpire Max O'Connell applied mouth-to-mouth resuscitation and I started breathing again. They rushed me to hospital, yet I was discharged that night to be back at the crease at the next fall of wicket the following morning."

Gallantly, Rick worked his way into the Australian team for the second Test against Pakistan in Perth in March 1979 scoring 75 and 79 and fielding with precision in the covers to win the Man of the Match award. Selection in the 1979 Australian World Cup team followed, but he struggled to make runs.

Daring to be denied, Rick bounced back again to make the Australian team for the Test tour of India, but injury and illness plagued his campaign. In the final Test in Mumbai, he was lured into a hook shot against a Kapil Dev bouncer that split his head open. Another hospital emergency!

The return of Australian players from World Series Cricket was bound to displace young players trying to establish their careers at the highest level. After 14 Test matches, Rick had scored 697 runs at an average of 26.8. Although he was not recalled to the strengthened Test side, he did go on to figure in the Australian one-day teams in 1979-1980 and again in 1981-1982, playing a total of 18 matches for 363 runs averaging 21.3.

The 1981-1982 season was one of his best for South Australia. He missed two Shield games on one-day duties for Australia but played for SA against the West Indies and Pakistan. In nine first class matches for SA he scored 1,011 runs at an average of 72. Skipper Hookes often said Rick's opening performances with Wayne Phillips helped pave the way for the team to win the Sheffield Shield that summer.

But the next summer literally shattered everything that Rick had built in cricket, especially his confidence. Against Queensland at Adelaide Oval, he was drawn into a hook shot against John Maguire. Rick's own words best explain the horrible moments of that delivery. "He got one to really rear up, and I moved back to hook. It went between the visor and the top part of the helmet and smashed into my eye socket. That finished me. After that, I didn't want to be there. I thought of other things I wanted to do in life. Even though I continued playing at Sheffield Shield level, the injury affected me deeply, and it still causes problems with my sight today."

Rick played in the Shield sides of 1983-1984, and again the following season, with a mix of success from a brave man who fought against the demons of injury.

His 98 first class matches yielded 5,554 runs at an average of 35.83.

Unfortunately, the repetitive battering at the crease left him with a condition called post-traumatic epilepsy causing spiralling dizzy spells. Medication has controlled the problem, but it still haunts the man who was without doubt thrown into the furnace of Test cricket prematurely.

"Yes, I would have liked more time to mature as a batsman before being called into the Test team, but I have no regrets," he said. "I gave it everything. One of my most cherished memories was playing in the Australian side with my idol Doug Walters, and we put on a partnership of 60-odd runs in a one-day international in Sydney. And Doug didn't mind the hook shot either."

1. The Old Holden

Waikerie, South Australia, 1969.

I t was summer in the Mid-Murray Cricket Association, stretching from Waikerie to Blanchetown as the river flows. The day was excruciatingly hot, but we did not care about the weather as it was for us a day off work or school to play sport. Life growing up on the river was idyllic. Waikerie Gold was my team, and we had to travel to Blanchetown, about 40 kilometres towards Adelaide.

Jon Mathews, more commonly called Jon, Pretty Boy, Roo Balls, Guts Mathews, was our captain and he was at the wheel of his two-toned blue 1960 FB Holden with a 'three on the tree' gear shift. Harry (Never Mind the Quality Feel the Width) Nethercliff, who bowled a nice little out-swinger, was in the front with Guts. Between them was a metal Esky full of the necessary refreshments.

Alan (Alley Cat) Kent, age 14, and myself, age 13, were in the back seat squashed up against a Labrador dog called Pluto, age unknown, who was salivating over my soggy fritz and tomato sandwich. Mum packed sandwiches for all of us along with a sponge cake for afternoon tea. In shorts as junior members of the team, the burning hot vinyl seat stuck to our thighs, slobber from the panting Pluto dripped onto our bare legs cooling us somewhat, and the hot wind blew in from the open window.

Alan McGilvray's distinctive commentary of the Test match flowed from the cheap after-market radio with staccato reception via a twisted wire coat hanger in the aerial socket. (Little did I know that Alan McGilvray and I would become good friends in the short years that followed).

Despite the windows being fully down, quarter windows extended and air vents open, the car was thick with plumes of cigarette smoke and the wafting aroma of Californian Poppy hair oil.

Marlboro Reds were the cigarettes of choice in the front seat with Guts and Never Mind the Quality Feel the Width sharing a 'King Brown' bottle of Southwark beer in preparation for the game. Ahead of his time in sports science, Guts, with tongue in cheek, advised the importance of "keeping your fluids up." In the back seat, Cat sipped on a warm Fanta, while I guzzled a Passiona. Pluto's rancid breath and horrendous farting contributed to the toxic air in our pre-match travel preparation for the showdown against Blanchetown.

There was a fair chance that with the heat and Guts's heavy foot, something would go wrong and, of course, it did! The steam coming from under the bonnet was a sure sign that the radiator had boiled, but there was good news and bad. The good news was that we limped to the patchy shade of the only mallee tree on the barren plain. The bad news was that we had no water to replenish the radiator.

However, the ever-reliable Guts came to the rescue. "Not a problem," he declared. As the motor cooled, he and Never Mind the Quality Feel the Width poured icy water from the Esky into Pluto's water bucket and placed it on the hot bitumen road to warm before refilling the radiator. Something told Cat and me that this predicament had presented itself before as it seemed to be well choreographed. We occupied ourselves with some fielding

practice in the dappled light of the mallee tree.

The FB Holden and its perspiring occupants made it to Blanchetown, and after stocking up with ice from the roadhouse, we made it just in time for the start of play with the remaining 'Long Necks' of beer nestling on ice in the Esky. Pluto, still panting from the heat flopped down under a river red gum amongst the ants.

I made my first century in that match after being dropped on nought. It was a defining day for me because if I had been caught and dismissed for a duck my sporting path may have taken a different turn. I had been juggling other sporting interests, that may have won out if I had failed in my first match as a 13-year-old playing against men.

Football was always my first sporting passion and I distinctly remember some four years later, Dad having a loud phone conversation with the legendary player and coach, Fos Williams. Fos wanted me to try out at West Adelaide as the Riverland, in that era, was West Adelaide's recruitment zone. However, in those days, fathers called the shots and, needless to say, I remained a cricketer. It was probably for the best as I was only a skinny kid and would have been easy fodder and crunched by the big men of the SANFL.

However, one of my fondest and proudest memories in sport was representing the Riverland Football Association against the Barossa and Light Football Association at the

Loxton Oval in 1975. I was named Best on Ground playing on the wing. Not long after that, I sustained a cracked skull on the Waikerie Oval against Loxton.

At about the same time I received a broken nose and shrapnel wounds to my face and eyes after a shooting accident courtesy of a surplus war rifle and old ammunition. This virtually finished my football career, at least at that level. My biggest problem when playing football was discipline where my fat mouth didn't endear me to the umpires and the opposition players. Athletics, as a sprinter, also had great appeal to me, but the logistics and lack of infrastructure for budding athletes was a concern.

To celebrate such a rewarding day at Blanchetown, Cat and I were allowed to sample the dregs of a Long Neck on the way home to Waikerie. Then, the three Waikerie teams would congregate at the local community club to dissect their games.

Jon Mathews was a handy country sportsman and coach. As coach of the Waikerie Senior Colts Football team, in which I was part, he had this theory of treating pulled muscles and other aches and pains. The idea was to apply a steaming hot towel for ten minutes followed by an ice pack for ten minutes to the affected area. This was done for two or three times or until you couldn't stand the pain any more. Jon thought his remedy must be working as less and less players presented with sore muscles. We were in fact in fear of the pain from his therapeutic cure. The second degree burns from the steam and ice certainly masked the pain of the muscles; however, the muscles made no improvement. His theory didn't last long.

Jon was way ahead of his time with his body art. He was the first person I saw with tattoos, which were quite rudimentary by today's standards. Apart from the art being displayed on his arms, it was common knowledge that some were on parts that probably should be left to the imagination.

Jon died in 2020. His love for all sports was infectious.

2. From ball to bat to friendship

Adelaide No 2 Oval, 1970.

n the 1970s, the only way a country kid could be recognised for bigger and better things was to be selected in a Combined Country Schoolboys team to play against the boys from each of the district cricket clubs during the Christmas school holidays. The country boys had to find their own accommodation or be billeted out. Fortunately, I had generous grandparents in the city who were very happy to have me stay with them during the carnival. However, finding my way to some of the unfamiliar grounds, via public transport, was a bit of a chore and a speedy learning experience.

Above all, as a country kid, it was a great adventure. I was one of those country kids who played in a three-week tournament known then as the Shell Shield. I was selected as a spin bowler who could bat a little bit. I had good figures with the ball up until we played West Torrens and one David Hookes. Hookesy was two years older than me, and he was brash, bold, street wise and

confident. When he drove to the ground as a man and I had to catch the bus as a boy, it was quite intimidating. You could see then that he was destined for big things. Hookesy took a liking to my bowling and smashed me to all corners of Adelaide No 2 Oval. However, I did manage to save face by making about 50 not out when I batted.

From that day on, I was marked as a batsman who couldn't bowl by so called 'coaches' at junior level who knew little about the game! This changed my outlook. To be stripped of the most enjoyable part of my game was shameful. I can never forgive those nameless 'control freaks' who were merely junior activity teachers. I didn't get another bowl ever, except for the Leagues in Lancashire 20 years later.

I played for two years in the country teams before SACA coach, Ernie Clifton, convinced me to join the Salisbury District Cricket Club. It was a pathway that opened up for me as an aspiring young cricketer and I spent a large portion of my district playing days with Salisbury.

The initial meeting with Hookesy developed into a great friendship. We played SA Schoolboys and SA Colts (Under-23) cricket together before he played his maiden First Class game for SA in October 1975. I was selected in the State team in December 1975, and we won the Sheffield Shield that season under Ian Chappell's captaincy. From the outset, I could see Hookesy moulding himself on Chappell, who was also our childhood idol.

It was overwhelming for me to play and go on tour with greats like Ian Chappell, Terry Jenner, Ashley Mallett, Gary Cosier, Wayne Prior and Ashley Woodcock. Yet Hookesy took it all in his stride. We both played for SA for the next 11 seasons. Hookesy and I shared a unit for a period and in the early 1980s I joined him at the West Torrens Cricket Club where he was captain. We won the Sheffield Shield again in 1981-1982 with Hookesy at the helm.

During my sporadic international cricketing career, I was honoured to play with and against the best cricketers in the world. Hookesy certainly fell within that category. Unfortunately, I didn't play any Test matches with Hookesy, but I did play two or three ODIs with him. I distinctly remember helping him off the plane in Adelaide after he badly pulled a hamstring while taking a catch against the West Indies in Sydney.

Hookesy was born on 3 May, and I was born on 1 May. For several years, we celebrated our birthdays together at the West Torrens Cricket Club while watching a local footy game. Hookesy loved his West Torrens Eagles and being with his mates. He had such a broad range of knowledge on most subjects, it seemed there were not enough hours in the day for all the things that he aspired to in life. Whether he was telling a joke at a bar or barbecue, addressing the players as captain, giving an after-dinner speech, or meeting royalty, he loved being the centre of attention.

He was a world class, talented cricketer and captain with an outstanding record.

Hookesy died tragically in 2004. Like so many others, I miss Hookesy and all the characteristics that made him such a good bloke.

3. "I'll fix it."

Cadell Oval, South Australia, 1972.

Waikerie Gold travelled about 25 kilometres to Cadell on a hot Saturday to play a team from the local low security prison. Most of the prisoners were good sportsmen, then maybe a few were just looking for a day out. Interaction between the prisoners and us was never a problem and always interesting.

A prisoner by the name of Howie Day, a tall athletic man, was batting. From the bowler's end, I signalled to Alan (Cat) Kent, our wicketkeeper, that the next ball would be a wrong 'un. Howie picked it up quickly and hitting with the spin, his slog went over the mid-wicket boundary into an irrigation channel far beyond the Athol Pines on the eastern side of the ground. The fast-flowing water in the channel swallowed up the ball and it was never seen again. It was the biggest hit that I have ever seen, but I did say to Howie how amazing it was to be able to hit a ball like that with his eyes closed! The next ball went nearly as far!

Before the game, one of my teammates, John (Bucky)

Buckskin, thought it prudent to lock his car considering the backgrounds of some members of our opposition. Unfortunately, he left his keys inside the car. We all tried to unlock the door, but only succeeded in scratching the glass and paintwork. The prison bus stopped nearby, and Bucky asked, "Any of you blokes know how to open a locked car?" The bus filled with laughter as Bucky realised what he had said. "I'll fix it," said one of the prisoners called 'Pigga' eager to hone his locksmithing skills. With a twist of the wire, and a gentle thump on a screwdriver, the lock popped open. All done in about ten seconds. Bucky showed his gratitude to Pigga with a pack of cigarettes, and everyone was happy, even the prison guards aboard the bus.

Bucky was an outstanding sportsman with mannerisms on the cricket field like that of Sir Garfield Sobers. He was an elegant left-handed batsman and could bowl genuine pace, then revert to spin. I have no doubt he could have played district cricket in Adelaide, and perhaps higher than that level. Bucky loved his football and became one of the Riverland's most brilliant players making the All-Australian Aboriginal Football Team, as did his brother Barry.

Bucky died in 2013.

In 2003, Cadell Oval was made redundant through team amalgamations and dwindling player numbers. The remnants of the cricket pitch, goal posts, netball courts and change rooms and are still recognisable and conjure up fine memories for many generations of sports people. It is now a sheep paddock as it was decades before.

4. Rookie

Adelaide Oval, South Australia, 1975.

The last sessions of Sheffield Shield and Test cricket used to be telecast on grainy, black and white television, which we eagerly watched at home in the Riverland. I had been to a few Test matches as a kid sitting on the terraces on the eastern side of Adelaide Oval while recording play in my treasured ABC scorebook. But I had never been to a Sheffield Shield game until I played in one. I was still living in Waikerie at the time of my first selection in the State team and I soon discovered the South Australian Cricket Association (SACA) had only a limited budget for transport and accommodation.

To make my Sheffield Shield debut, I caught the country to city bus from Waikerie with a small suitcase and my cricket gear. The bus dropped me at Gepps Cross, a long hike from Adelaide, and I caught another bus to the even more distant Tea Tree Gully Hotel Motel, where the SACA had decided to put up the 17-year-old kid from the country. Perhaps it was a hint that I should find my own accommodation in the future. This, while during games and other functions, board members, committee members and the like, had their snouts buried deep in the trough. My teammates were appalled at this treatment, but not surprised.

Practice was scheduled the next day and, with very little money in my pocket, I was on the bus again, this time to town, followed by a walk with my gear to Adelaide Oval. I arrived in footy shorts, T-shirt and thongs, with my cricket gear in a small kit bag, and suddenly found myself alongside my childhood heroes including Ian Chappell as captain and Ashley Mallett as vice-captain.

That afternoon I walked around Adelaide eventually finding the store of sports distributor, Dave Parkinson, on Halifax Street. Dave was very generous and presented me with a brand-new Gray Nicholls bat and a quality Puma black and yellow tracksuit with matching shoes. (There was no such thing as state colours in those days). I was very appreciative and treasured them. In fact, I had the 'trackie pants' for about 40 years before my wife threw them out. A testimony to good quality. I developed a long-standing friendship with Dave Parkinson and his fast-bowler son, Sam, who became my State teammate. After the memorable meeting with Dave, I boarded another bus back to the Tea Tree Gully Hotel Motel to bathe my blisters and to study the bus schedule to get me back to Adelaide Oval by 9.30am the following day for my Sheffield Shield debut.

In those days, there was no hat or blazer presentation for a new player. However, I was given a cap and told it was the only one until it wore out, the same rule applied to the sleeveless jumper. If I wanted a long sleeve jumper, I had to pay for it. The user pays rule also applied to all our other clothing and equipment, unless you were a big-name player and received a contract through one of the cricketing brands. Our non-stretch shirts and trousers (which was like playing in a suit by today's standards) were proudly displayed on coat hangers on arrival at the ground, and then, at the end of the day, unceremoniously stuffed into a bag for overnight washing and pressing. The coat hanger show was also the normal at grade cricket level, even down to D-grade. In fact, it wasn't long before my time that club blazers had to be worn to the various grounds and then donned again for social drinks after the game.

The preamble to the game was merely a quick net, if you wanted to, a cup of tea, a joke, then into it. I wore my favourite white towelling floppy hat (mum whipped it up on her sewing machine) until the red caps became the norm. The only thing that I clearly remember about that first innings was walking out to bat at number five in my floppy hat, taking guard and looking up to see Jeff Thomson at the top of his mark. They were the days of eight ball overs and the umpire yelled, "Right arm over with six to come." I had been warned that a yorker, or the bouncer would be first up. The first ball I faced was a yorker that I managed to jam down with my new bat and squeezed the ball to square leg for a single.

I was run out for five runs in that first innings, and in my last innings for South Australia twelve years later I was run out for 10. Some people reckon I should have worked on my running between wickets, while others say the batsmen at the other end should have worked on theirs.

The four-day match payment was $20 before tax with each player contributing $1 of his payment to show our gratitude to Bob McDonald, who was our room steward.

Bob went far and beyond his duty statement, to the point where he used to arrive at the ground extra early and line up all our boots on a drop sheet. With an old paint brush, he would make our boots look like new with a watered down white paint slurry. He would then place them in front of our locker ready for the day's play. He would also do our pads, on request, if they were the canvas style. Bob certainly deserved his extra $12. Not begrudging Bob and the other ground staff in any way, they were getting paid more than the players. No wonder Ian Chappell and the other senior players were more than disgruntled with the state of affairs.

We won the Sheffield Shield that year despite some internal controversy and even a strike.

After my early lodgings at the Tea Tree Gully Hotel Motel, I stayed with State and Test fast bowler, Wayne (Fang) Prior, and his family in Elizabeth.

As a rookie, the presence of Sir Donald Bradman, who used to frequent the change rooms as a Board Member, was a jaw dropping experience for me. I mean how often do you get to meet a man of his fame who was nearly twice as good as any other batsman, and probably will be forever. After a few nervous attempts at conversation by me I soon relaxed and found that he was quite happy to talk golf, gardening, or family. I think he welcomed the respite from talking cricket.

5. Damn seagulls!

Adelaide Oval, 1975.

Terry Jenner (TJ) came to Adelaide from Perth in the early 1970s to take advantage of the wickets that were more suited to his bowling.

TJ wasn't the fittest of first-class players. Fitness in the seventies was gained from either match play or net practice. Extra running or gym work were non-existent. I can still picture in my mind TJ relaxing in the rooms at a break in play telling a story with a smoke and a cup of tea, with his trademark smile on his face.

He would normally field in the gully, and I was nearby in the covers, a fielding position I held for my entire career. TJ was never keen on chasing the ball when it was hit between the two of us. Even before the ball came anywhere near either of us, he would yell out, "You go!" The nickname 'Hugo' stuck until he retired in the late 1970s.

TJ had a very good bowling action and on his delivery stride, his head would point to the sky with his mouth wide open.

Seagulls have always called the hallowed turf of Adelaide Oval their toilet. In one very memorable delivery, TJ opened his 'gob' skyward, and a seagull dropped its business right into his mouth. A few dry retches later, and multiple glasses of lemon cordial to dilute any goo left in his mouth, play resumed, but not before everyone had a smart comment. The best comment was from Ian Chappell, who snapped, "TJ you have always talked a lot of shit!" Ashley (Rowdy) Mallett, the great Australian off-spinner, was in a spasm of laughter. Many said that afterwards when TJ laughed it was more like a squawk.

Most of us were more wary of the seagulls from then on, but the broad brimmed hat offered some protection. I don't know of any other another cricket ground where seagulls congregate in such a confined area right behind the bowler's arm. I would often talk to myself when facing a ball, "Don't watch the seagulls, don't watch the seagulls!" But sometimes no matter how hard I tried I still looked at them, a very unwelcome distraction when facing the likes of Jeff Thomson.

Trudging off the field after losing my wicket from such a distraction, that was my excuse anyway, the seagulls would be squawking especially loudly, as if to say, "Got you again!" I often wish that I could get to the 12-gauge shotgun that is proudly displayed, but safely locked, away only metres away from the change rooms.

The gun was used by security guards to protect the

pitch from overnight vandals during the early part of the 20th century. Some of the seagulls may have met their fate during this time.

TJ, although he probably wasn't the ideal role model for me as an aspiring cricketer, was truly a lovable larrikin. It was a different cricket culture in that era and was seen as the norm.

TJ died in 2011.

6. From strike to the Sheffield Shield

Adelaide, 1976.

STATE CRICKETERS QUIT.
NEW TEAM TO BE PICKED TODAY.

These headlines were on the front page of Adelaide's morning newspaper, *The Advertiser*, on Tuesday 24 February 1976. We were a heartbeat away from winning the Sheffield Shield that season.

A row had broken out between our senior players and the selectors over some individuals who were picked, or not picked, for the final two games of the season in Sydney and Brisbane. South Australia had just beaten Victoria, and the younger players, who were not directly involved in the row, respected and unanimously supported the protest actions of the senior players in our team.

Our captain, Ian Chappell, had for years been fighting for better pay and conditions for players, and along with the selection issue, was pushed to his limits. His requests had always produced a negative response from the hierarchy, and he was tired of it.

The SACA selectors would not budge on the selection issue, and they were adamant that the team they had chosen would remain. Ultimately, we decided that winning the Sheffield Shield that season was the best way of 'sticking it up' the hierarchy. Ian and the other senior players agreed and respected the fact that the younger players in the team did not want to have their commitment and records tarnished. The gesture from our senior players effectively ended the threat of a strike.

After taking full points from the game against Victoria, we only had to draw one of the next two games to win the Sheffield Shield. It turned out to be an anti-climax to the season as a two-day washout in Sydney effectively gave us the draw we needed. A two-and-a-half-day washout in Brisbane was a dead rubber and the official end of the season.

Ashley (Rowdy) Mallett was our man for comical relief during those rainy days in Sydney and Brisbane that were otherwise spent reading, playing cards, drinking tea, and generally messing around in the rooms. There was no such thing as indoor nets for practice and passing the time. Having won the Shield, we were all keen to get home to our families to celebrate.

However, in Brisbane the umpires insisted on waiting for conditions to improve so that a start could be

made. Late on the third day, the match finally began, and we were fielding. Rowdy, in his own witty way, made it known that he wasn't too happy about being out there by rolling his pants up past his knees as if he were playing in a swamp. One by one, we followed suit. Then Rowdy took his shoes and socks off to drive home his message to the umpires. Threats of reports for dissent were made clear by the umpires, but we did make some exaggerated fielding attempts, as if to avoid injury on the sloppy surface, before the next thunderstorm effectively ended the game. Rowdy had earned another nickname, 'The Swamp Fox' courtesy of Geoff Attenborough.

Ashley (Rowdy) Mallett died in 2021

It was a well-deserved Sheffield Shield victory, and I was proud to be part of a team that consisted of Chappell, Mallett, Jenner, Attenborough, Prior, Cosier, Woodcock, Curtin, Hookes, Yagmich, Hogg and Blewett, and of course others throughout the season.

Celebrations were endless as each sponsor had a function for us, along with the SACA, the State Government and the City of Adelaide. Many hotels and wineries were also keen to be part of it all. Ian was a great public speaker and always said the right things with plenty of humour. He couldn't resist a dig at those who deserved it. Mainly the cricket administrators and the press.

The negative press that we received due to the threatened strike created a strong sense of unity in the side that I will always remember. It is often difficult to get people in a team to integrate on and off the field, but when it happens it creates something special. If a coach could manufacture such unity, it would be a highly sought-after product.

I was there again in the Sheffield Shield winning team of 1981-1982 and served as a selector in the Shield win in of 1995-1996. The SACA Sheffield Shield trophy cabinet hasn't been opened since then.

7. Chappell v Lillee

Perth, 1976.

Two of South Australia's legendary captains were Les (Favelli) Favell and Ian (Chappelli) Chappell. Respectfully, I called them Les and Ian. It didn't seem to be that long ago when I was calling them Mr Chappell and Mr Favell.

For our Perth trip, Les was team manager and selector. We arrived in time for practice on the day prior to the game starting. It was hot, and as always, not a drop of rain.

Saturday night was traditionally set aside for the Gloucester Park trots over the road from the WACA, and on this occasion we were entertained by the hierarchy of the trotting club. Les was a keen gambler (as were Mallett, Jenner, Prior, Hookes and Curtin), and after studying the form guide, we found a few winners. I didn't mind a flutter on the horses to get into the spirit of the night, but soon found that I liked my money too much.

The first three days of the game paved the way for us

to chase a total in the last innings to win the game. Until that stage of my career, I had batted in the middle order, but things were about to change. I was notoriously nervous prior to batting, an issue Les and Ian identified. Unbeknown to me, a decision was made about where I would bat. Les came to me just before the start of our run chase and said in his typically gruff fashion, "Righto son, put the pads on, you're opening." I certainly wasn't going to argue with greats like Les and Ian, so out I went with Ashley (Splinter) Woodcock to face the opening bowlers. Splinter was out early, then out strode Ian, full of swagger and confidence, to start antagonising the Western Australian boys. This was a tactic Ian used to get his adrenalin pumping, plus he liked a laugh. On this occasion, Dennis Lillee was in his firing line. They were mates when playing for Australia, but when in opposition, they were full-on adversaries.

Typically, the 'Fremantle Doctor' was blowing hard from the south-west and, of course, Lillee was bowling with it. As a compulsive hooker of the short ball, I knew I could expect a few to rough me up. I didn't have to wait long! Luckily, I managed a few hook shots for fours and sixes. Ian then 'went to town' verbally on Dennis, and more bouncers came at both of us. The great fast bowler was fuming, and Ian got into him even more.

At one stage, he fronted Dennis, chest to chest, and said words to the effect of, "Come on, mate, you can do better than that. He is just a kid." I then gingerly approached

Ian and said, "Shut the hell up, I don't need him to bowl any quicker. My life is in danger." (Keep in mind that helmets, chest guards, arm guards and improvements to gloves and pads, etc. were still a decade away. A few folded hankies in the pocket was deemed suffice as a thigh pad). It didn't stop Ian, who was having the time of his life. He said to me, "This is a good initiation for you boy!" My sarcastic reply was, "Gee whiz, thanks for that" A few more top edges and some off the middle of the bat saw us win the game with time to spare.

Ian awarded me the Man of the Match prize, a mustard brown bedside flip alarm clock, which was fashionable at the time. As one of my nicknames was 'Midnight', it was an appropriate award. The name Midnight was given to me by a long serving SACA employee and Junior Cricket Coordinator, Ray Sutton. I tended to catch a snooze whenever I could. So, the name Midnight stuck while Ray was involved. I still have the clock today, but it no longer keeps the time.

Ian will always be my hero. Les died in 1987.

8. Big Clacka

Salisbury Oval, South Australia, 1976.

The Salisbury District Cricket Club was admitted to the South Australian Cricket Association district competition in season 1965-1966, and for many years it was one of the 'easy beats'.

However, a strong club was developed through the recruitment of players like Graham (Clacka) Clarke, Gary Wright and Wayne Prior and the strong foundations established by Bob Zadow, Wayne Bradbrook, Barry Causby, David Patrick, and John Alexander. The 'up-and-comers' were John Davey, Glenn Bishop and Harvey Jolly. These players, alongside other key contributors, saw Salisbury win the A-grade Premiership under the captaincy of Clacka in 1976-1977.

Over the next 15 years, Salisbury won nine premierships becoming the 'measuring stick' for the other teams in the competition. Club stalwarts including Kevin Angel, Ernie Clifton, Trevor Jarman, Geoff Daly, George Candy and Hartley Wood, some of whom played in 1965-1966, were integral to the success of the club.

During that first premiership year, I was travelling from Waikerie to play each weekend although State commitments had started to take over. My cousins from Waikerie, Wayne and Donn Darling, also played A-grade for Salisbury that year. We trained together on the Ramco hard wickets during the week, coaching each other, bowling and throwing balls until our arms almost fell off. The time I spent practising with them and my father was the sole reason I progressed to higher levels.

Two of my friends from Waikerie, Byron (Big) Gregory and Lester (Leroy) Lawrie also played at the Salisbury club. They trained with the Darlings during the week providing a variety of bowling with Big a fast bowler and Leroy a leg spinner. Later, as my career progressed, formal coaching for me was non-existent, even though so-called coaches were paid a lot of money for being little more than practice timekeepers. Even today I very rarely see a so-called coach get hands-on with a player.

Clacka was a huge man who bowled left arm medium fast. His special combination was a slow bouncer, followed by a much quicker throat ball that gave an unwary batsman a lot of grief. He was also a more than accomplished middle order batsman with a physique that made the bat look like a toothpick in his hands.

Clacka was noted for his thirst on a hot day, and I

distinctly remember a match against Woodville on the Salisbury Oval with the temperature soaring. (It always seemed to be a few degrees hotter at Salisbury than any other ground). Clacka enjoyed a couple of 'secret' ales to freshen up at tea and, continuing to bowl after the break, he put a little extra grunt into one of his deliveries which followed through in more ways than one. He then had to hurriedly leave the field for a shower and a clean pair of pants. Clacka always carried a spare pair of pants, and some reckoned he needed more in his bag. He would always use this time to check on the race results and relay them to the interested punters.

Every club had its stout-hearted characters. Clacka was ours at Salisbury, and Woodville had Mick Clingley. Walking off the ground at the end of day's play, there was a bit of sledging between Wayne Darling and Mick, which led to a bit of argy bargy. Donn Darling, never one to be shy, jumped on Mick's back and rode him like a rodeo bull. Hurriedly, Clacka positioned his big frame (clean pants and all) between the rivals to settle things down, and he made sure that everyone had a beer together afterwards.

One of Clacka's favourite on-field tricks, when things got a bit mundane, was to set up, in collusion with the batsman, a fake catch to fine leg. Clacka would pretend to bowl a bouncer and the batsman would pretend to play a hook shot. Clacka would then call out catch, catch. The fine leg fieldsman would be looking in the air and running around frantically for the ball that wasn't there. Meanwhile Clacka would roll the ball along the ground in the vicinity of the fieldsman where he realised that a catch had gone begging. The rest of the team would stand there with hands on hips, shaking their heads in pretence. Clacka had it down to a fine art and it was always good for a laugh.

To reciprocate for Salisbury's hospitality to the Darling boys, Wayne, Donn and me, we used to invite the club to our properties in the Riverland for end of season trips, usually around Easter time. It was an eye opener for some of the city boys who enjoyed the opportunity to go water skiing, spotlighting and trail biking. A game between Salisbury players and the locals provided many laughs with a barbecue and beverages an integral part of proceedings. Visits to the local pub were also on the agenda during these trips.

Clacka played six first-class games for South Australia and was a member of Salisbury's Team of the 20th century. He died in 2006

9. A Long Way for a Game of Cricket

Waikerie, Adelaide, Sydney, San Francisco, New York, Puerto Rico and St Kitts, 1978.

Prior to starting the biggest adventure of my life, I was water skiing on the Murray River at the popular Holder Bend Ski Beach, Waikerie. Now, nobody would dispute that my father had a loud booming voice, so when I heard it from the other side of the river, coming from a cloud of dust which had originated from a skidding utility, I swam across to investigate.

He said, "Jump in, you have to go to Adelaide."

I could tell that he was a bit anxious and eager to get me away from the ski beach, because my injury proneness was becoming well entrenched, and skiing wasn't the safest of sports. I assume, someone would have picked up my thongs and towel but that was the last I saw of them. Two days later I was playing in my first Test match.

After the Adelaide Test we quickly assembled at the Australian Cricket Board office which was literally a couple of small offices up a narrow staircase off George Street, Sydney. It was our final briefing before the tour of the West Indies. It was the beginning of a very eventful and concerning period.

Immediately after a 17-hour flight to San Francisco we learnt that the Sydney Hilton Hotel, where we had stayed at the previous night, had been bombed with three people killed and 11 injured. It was obviously big news in Australia, and the story made the front page of some American papers. At that time, connecting flights were not readily available and we had nearly twenty hours to kill before our next leg to New York. A tour bus was organised for a day out and we were amazed at the grandeur of the Golden Gate Bridge and spectacular harbour of San Francisco. It was a great day providing the opportunity for players to get to know one another.

Six hours onward to New York and we were stretching our legs outside the airport terminal in falling snow. Coming from the heat of the Australian summer to freezing conditions in New York was a big contrast. Then we were confronted with the heat and humidity of the West Indies.

Inside the terminal in New York, we started a two-up game led by Jeff (Two Up) Thomson. It must have been Thommo's speciality as he had this nickname well before the Windies tour. In typical Aussie fashion, the noise was building as money was won and lost on flips of a coin. Soon, two burly New York Police Department cops rolled up to control the raucous behaviour. However, they were so intrigued by the game they quickly joined in for a bit of fun, without betting on duty, of course!

The onward journey was a five-hour flight aboard an American Airlines jumbo to San Juan in Puerto Rico. We filed down one of the aisles to the back of the plane where I expected we would all be sitting together. But that is not quite how things worked out, much to the amusement of the lads. In the middle seat next to me was a huge West Indian woman with her baby in the aisle seat. At that time I was a skinny lad and there I was pressed hard up against the window with her billowing body spilling over the armrest. That was only the beginning of a very uncomfortable flight. Then the unthinkable happened, the hungry baby needed breast-feeding and I didn't know which way to look, pressed harder up against the window and hardly able to breathe, the smart remarks and giggles from my Aussie teammates made my face go even redder. After the baby settled, the woman and I shared an interesting conversation in which she said she was amused with the accents and antics of the Australian cricketers.

In San Juan, we learnt that for the next three months employees of British Airways and Caribbean Airways would be on strike. We were all getting a little grumpy by this stage as our smallpox vaccinations, coupled with jet lag, were starting to take effect. Charter aircraft were organised, ageing propeller 'jalopies', in which we fitted

luggage and ourselves as best we could. That was the norm of air travel for the next three months, but flying at much lower altitudes than usual gave us a great view of the Caribbean islands and ocean beneath.

Initially, our flight was to Basseterre on the island of St Kitts where we were to begin our playing campaign. Before our first game, we enjoyed two days of rest and recreation at a beautiful, converted plantation house surrounded by sugar cane and pineapple trees. The beach beckoned, and the sand, surprisingly, was a volcanic jet black in stark contrast to the blue and turquoise of the water.

A refreshing swim in the warm Caribbean water along with a rum punch and the sounds of steel drums resonating, was the perfect way to end nearly five days of travel. Welcome to paradise!

10. Ripped Off

St George's, Grenada, West Indies, 1978.

t is hard to avoid the beach in the West Indies. The warm weather brings tourists, and the tourists attract unscrupulous opportunists. One such opportunist saw us as an easy target. Jeff (Thommo) Thomson, Gary (Cos) Cosier, Ian (Mad Dog) Callen, Fred Bennett our manager, and I were content on the beach, swimming in the surf and throwing around a frisbee. However, Graeme (Wally) Yallop couldn't resist the temptation to see what the conmen were up to. They worked in groups among the food and souvenir stalls, and their sleight of hand tricks were always quite convincing. The card gamers, and the dice magicians in particular, were always a good way to lose a couple of dollars in amazement.

Wally was back in a flash trying to find his wallet to take advantage of the 'unbelievable' deal being offered. Minutes later he proudly returned showing us his 'once-in-a-lifetime' purchase of a brand-new Omega gold watch

– one of the most expensive and prestigious timepieces of the era.

It really was a beautiful looking watch, but as Wally soon found out that was the only good thing about it. Upon closer inspection the minute hand had been strategically placed over the g in Omega. When the minute hand moved around it revealed that the g was actually c, which made Wally the proud owner of an unknown Omeca watch.

We all had a good laugh. Wal, with typical level-headedness, laughed it off as a lesson learnt at minimal cost. As we had a bit of muscle in the group with Thommo and Mad Dog we decided to track down the hustler to quiz him about his spelling skills. We soon thought better of it as the conman's associates had much bigger biceps than ours.

I'm not sure how long the watch lasted, but from then if anyone wanted to know the time, they had to ask 'The Omeca Man'.

Mad Dog, who always had something smart to say, told Wal, "You are not going to 'time' your cover drives any better with that watch."

Wal was one of my favourite batsmen, and highly underrated at national level. His record for Victoria is amongst the best. He played the ball late when defending or attacking, and in my opinion, is the hallmark of a good batsman. He is a good friend.

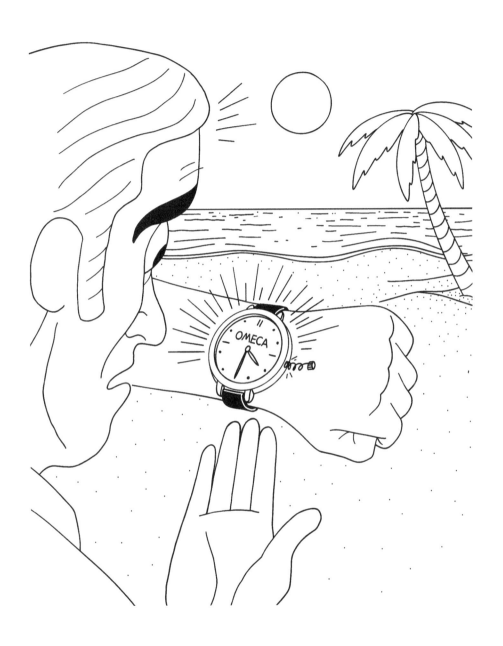

Wal wasn't the only one who fell victim to the lure of the quick dollar salesman. Most of us succumbed to the temptation of buying the mandatory five T-shirts for three dollars all depicting marijuana in some way – none of which survived the first wash. In a street market in Antigua, I couldn't resist two packets of Super 8 home movie film. It was a mystery purchase because I didn't have a movie camera or a projector, although from memory the plan was to buy them at some stage. It also didn't occur to me that Beta and VHS technology would soon take over in the world of recording home movies

The Super 8 tapes still go out on the table every time I have a garage sale. I remain a keen market shopper and still get ripped off. But it's all good fun.

11. Hilton Respite

Port of Spain, Trinidad, West Indies, 1978.

The Trinidad Hilton was the base for the team as we would return there on numerous occasions whether in transit or to play in the first and fourth Tests. It was by far the best hotel we stayed at during the three months touring the West Indies. In fact, it was then rated in the top ten of the best hotels in the world, and well ahead of it's time We looked forward to this respite from some of the other ordinary accommodation that we had elsewhere.

The Trinidad Hilton was perched high on a hill overlooking Port of Spain Harbour and surrounded by tropical rainforests. Because of its elevation, the hotel was a cool retreat after the heat and humidity of the city and the Queen's Park Cricket Ground below. All the first-class amenities were at the hotel including restaurants, pools, bars, movie theatre, casino, disco, golf, gym, and even a shopping centre. It really was a small town. There was no need to go out and, anyway, we were advised not to go into the city at night.

Travelling with us was the legendary cricket commentator, Alan McGilvray. At the time he was 69 years old, yet he certainly kept up with us young blokes. Also with the touring party were Australian cricket writers Alan Shiell, John Benaud, John Coomber, Phil Wilkins, Peter McFarlane and 'Keg' McKenzie, our photographer.

When staying at the Hilton, Alan McGilvray always arranged a room with an adjoining lounge. We soon found out why!

Alan's initiation, to those who hadn't had the pleasure, was to invite a group of lads up to his lounge for a drink. He would then open a bottle of brandy and throw the top out the window as if to say, "Let's finish it." We were all sure that it was his way of gleaning some inside stories to talk about on radio and write about in the press. It turned out to be a two-way street, as he told many fantastic stories from his 50 years in the media. As we all learnt later, Alan would have a tipple even if we were there or not.

Alan McGilvray died in 1996.

All the media men were fantastic people who joined in on all our social functions and other commitments. In fact, Alan Shiell from Adelaide gave me a great piece of coaching advice having played first class cricket for South Australia. (Sadly, that advice came too late in the

tour for me). The media men were never intrusive and always approachable. We included them when we could. It was three months of a marvellous association.

One evening after arriving back from the ground, a party was in progress around the pool. From memory it was a closed party, but some of us found our way in. Mingling in the crowd we noticed the host only a few metres away. After his courteous, cool nod of the head, I responded with something that resembled a nod, or was it a nervous twitch, while I morphed into a shrinking violet. It was no real big deal at the time as he was just another member of a family band. Later in this man's career he was crowned the unofficial King of Pop and regarded as one of the most significant cultural figures of the 20th century. He was 19-year-old Michael Jackson!

As the only white faces in the crowd, it was soon suggested by the bouncers that we move on.

Because of the Hilton Hotel's reputation and its noted clientele, it was the sought-after hotel in the West Indies by celebrities from all over the world.

12. Wrestling

Bridgetown, Barbados, West Indies, 1978.

There was an unwritten rule that if you returned to the hotel late at night you must be respectful of your roommate's rest.

On one such occasion I disobeyed that rule with Graeme (Baz) Wood. I was loud and full of bad manners after having savoured a few local rum punches. Before long a playful wrestling match broke out between us. Clumsily I fell and hit my head on the sharp corner of a coffee table. Blood flowed from a cut on my right ear. Baz felt quite proud of himself and didn't show any concern before going back to bed. I fell asleep on the couch.

The next morning, I awoke with the side of my head stuck to the pillow in dried blood. Gaining no sympathy nor assistance from Baz, I had no choice but to set off holding the bloodied pillow to my head, much to the amusement of other guests in the lobby and a standing ovation from my teammates. My plan was to immerse my head in the warm waters of the Caribbean. Eventually the dried blood softened, and the pillow came away from my ear.

The result was three stitches and a permanent indentation on my ear, plus I think the cost of the spoiled pillow was added to my hotel bill. Our captain, Bob (Simmo) Simpson thought it best that I do a few extra laps at training that morning.

It seemed that these wrestling matches between Australian cricketers had been popular well before my time as highlighted by Douglas K. Darling in his book about the life and times of his father, Joe Darling. The book is titled *Test Tussles On and Off the Field* with a foreword written by Sir Donald Bradman.

Sir Donald said in part, "One of the great names in Australian cricket history is Joe Darling. In fact, he was more than a great name; he was a legendary figure, a dynamic leader, a forthright and outstanding character, and a truly wonderful son of this country.

Some people still believe Joe Darling's 1902 side that toured England was the greatest Australian team ever to tread a cricket field." Joe toured England in 1896, 1899, 1902 and 1905.

As a boy I would often stare at a grainy photograph in our lounge room of Joe Darling posing in his cricket stance. It was an inspiration for me. Joe features in one of the branches of our family tree and it made me proud

to be associated with this great man of Australian cricket, farming and politics. I can only surmise that in his free time he got to know his wife, Alice, a bit better as they did have fifteen children.

Douglas Darling wrote, "Although Joe is of medium size, he is compactly and firmly built. When Ernie Jones came into the South Australian team and found his legs, so to speak, he was very keen after a bath to wrestle with the other chaps in the altogether. Ernie was a big, powerful chap and had been a Broken Hill miner. He was top dog at the wrestling business, and the fun was all his way until Joe Darling came into the team. Upon Ernie turning his gentle attention to Joe, he found himself and his teammate waltzing around the room for some time, each struggling to get the right grasp on the other, until finally the originator of this form of after-cricket pastime found himself sliding on his back into the corner where the showers were located. That cured Ernie of his wrestling habit and after that, peace always reigned in the dressing room."

A few generations later, the friendly skirmishes between Baz and me became a common pastime as we roomed together. We both knew after the 'Barbados Brawl' that injury could strike again. Of course, it did! Two years later in Kanpur, India, we were both bathed in sweat with beds up-turned, furniture broken, and profanities spat. I unleashed a series of poorly executed wrestling moves that resulted in Baz hitting his forehead on the plastered wall. "There you are," I said, "Remember Barbados."

The only medical man we had on tour was a masseuse and he was summoned to stem the bleeding. The only antiseptic he could find was after-shave lotion, which worked a treat and left Baz well perfumed. Not having a team doctor, or at very least a first aid kit – in India of all places – was very different from the medical staffing for the Australian team today.

13. Froth and Bubbles

Barbados, West Indies. 1978

There was only one thing to do on a rest day in Barbados and that was to hit the water. So, our wicket-keeper Steve (Stumpa) Rixon along with Baz, Bruce (Roo) Yardley and I hired a Mini Moke. That poor old Mini Moke seemed to go, or was made to go, faster and brake harder than what it was designed for. The intention was to go to the beach to do some snorkelling at a reef just offshore.

Roo gazed over the calm water wondering how we could get out to the reef. Nobody told us that at low tide we could walk there, but at high tide it was under three metres of water. A small row boat was anchored about one hundred metres from the beach, so off we swam. The boat served its purpose and took us another four hundred metres to the reef with spear guns waving around dangerously.

After a brief look around under the water, I climbed aboard the boat for a rest. Baz and Stumpa were holding

onto the side of the boat and Roo was swimming underwater not far away. "Watch this," I said to Baz and Stumpa before I took a deep breath and dived in. Stumpa and Baz were watching just below the water line as I swam up from behind Roo and grabbed his calf muscle digging my fingernails in and pulling hard.

The sea erupted into froth and bubbles from all parts of Roo's shocked body fearing a shark had attacked him. Baz, Stumpa and I could hardly control our laughter, taking in gulps of seawater and adding to the froth and bubbles. Roo finally saw the funny side of it, even though earlier I could have caught the sharp end of his spear gun. Roo was a bit reluctant to enter the water again for the rest of the tour.

It was a great experience, but reality soon set in as we faced the scornful face of the rightful owner of the boat. Everything turned out fine especially when a few free tickets to the cricket were presented. We then feared that the owner didn't realise that we tied his boat up to the wrong bouy. We sped off in the Moke not looking back. Finally, the trip back to the hotel in the Moke was a bit sobering as we contemplated playing the West Indies the next day with their fearsome fast bowling attack.

Apart from our skipper, Bob Simpson, Roo was the oldest player in our touring party at the age of 31. But we called him the world's oldest teenager because he was into everything. We all loved his company, and he was a very fine cricketer. Starting his career as a fast bowler he then changed to off spin to preserve his spindly body. He was more than an accomplished batsman and a dynamic gully fieldsman. As an aside, he was aptly nicknamed after a roo dog, as he was all prick and ribs!

Bruce Yardley died in 2020.

My wife of 38 years. Tania

Australian One Day International Team 1982

WAIKERIE GOLD — PREMIERS 1970-1971

STANDING: P. Wilson, K. Morley, L. Lawrie, J. Sutton, M. Darling, B. Brooks, R. Darling.
SITTING: J. Buckskin (Vice-Capt.), A. Steinert (Capt.), J. Matthews.

Murray Vale Studio

Where it all started. Waikerie Gold Cricket Team. 1970-71

KID FROM THE BUSH HITS THE BIG TIME

PUNK hovered behind the tin wicket waiting for a snick . . . but none came.

Fieldsmen Crumby and Bub moved in slow motion under the burning Waikerie sun, shielding their eyes to watch South Australia's wonderboy of cricket, Rick Darling, crack another ball into the orchards.

Darling, a cheeky-faced blond-haired 18-year-old, was facing the bowling of his father, Max, as he sharpened his batting eye for his first Sheffield Shield appearance against Greg Chappell's Queenslanders at Adelaide Oval tomorrow.

The daily lunchtime bush "Tests" have been part of Rick's build-up to top class cricket since he scored an unbeaten 43 for the SA Colts against the West Indies a fortnight ago.

Picture by DENNIS ROGERS.

● "The Darling of Waikerie"— full story, more pictures, Page 86.

● **Four more SA cricket stars** reported—Page 88

● **Shield game of the year,** says Richie Benaud—Page 86

Lunch time cricket at work 1975. Razor at short mid off,
Mud is the wicket keeper and Dad is the bowler.

One Day International v West Indies SCG 1982

The moment of triumph. South Australia have hit the winning run against Victoria and the Shield is bound for Adelaide. David Hookes, Rick Darling and Andrew Sincock lead a delirious dressing-room gallery. Photo: MILTON WORDLEY.

Winning the Sheffield Shield 1981-81

*Good Mate
Graeme Wood*

Winning Sheffield Team 1975-76

*Batting with Ian Chappell
v Victoria 1976*

Joe Darling. Australian Cricket Captain,
"Wrestler" and Inspiration.

Hooking v England
Adelaide Oval 1979.
Ian Botham in the
background.

Good mates on tour. David Hookes, Myself,
Wayne Phillips and Sam Parkinson

Pull shot v India,
Adelaide Oval 1978

My family and only coaches. Brook, Donn, Lindsay,
Wayne and my father Max Darling

My first Ball in Test Cricket v Indian Adelaide Oval 1978

Walking out to open the batting with Graeme Wood v India
Our first Test, Adelaide Oval 1978

How Graeme Wood and I used to run between wickets ... Graeme on the left.

Hook shot SA v Victoria MCG, 1976. Alan Hurst is the bowler.

Quite a funny cartoon on how some people view selectors.

Police escort for Aussies...
Riot after Test dismissal

KINGSTON, Jamaica: Rioting spectators today halted the Fifth cricket Test at Sabina Park as Australia were on the verge of beating the West Indies.

About 100 police and security men — many of them wearing helmets and carrying riot shields — were called onto the field as the crowd threw bottles, chairs, and large pieces of rock onto the ground.

The Australian team remained on the field, protected by a cordon of police, for 15 minutes before they ran to the dressing rooms.

As they sprinted to safety several bottles were hurled at them and the Australian players had been injured.

The match erupted when Vanburn Holder was given out caught behind off leg spinner Jim Higgs.

That sent the West Indies to nine for 258, and within one wicket of defeat with six overs and two balls of the match remaining.

Holder apparently did not think he had hit the ball and stood his ground for some seconds looking at umpire Wesley Malcolm, who had given him out.

Before the last batsman, Raphick Jumadeen, was half way to the wicket, the bottles and rocks began raining onto the field.

The bottle and rock throwing continued for nearly half an hour, and more than an hour after play had been stopped it was decided to abandon play for the day.

The crowd was clearly protesting the umpire's decision.

There was widespread bitterness in Jamaica and throughout the Caribbean when umpire Douglas Sang Hue was not appointed to officiate in this test.

He was initially nominated, but the West Indies Cricket Board of Control decided to withdraw the nomination following a protest from the Australians, who were unhappy with his umpiring in the First Test in Trinidad two months ago.

As the players left the field there were chants of "We want Sang Hue, we want Sang Hue", and more rocks and bottles were thrown, along with some iron chairs and other missiles.

Police moved in to disperse the crowd by firing blank ammunition from revolvers.

The sound of the shots sent the crowd scurrying back beneath the stands.

One man attempted to dig up the wicket with a knife and a piece of wood.

He dug a small hole inside the popping crease at the southern end.

Simpson said he had been told that a woman in the crowd put it out, and there was no real damage.

"None of our boys were hit by bottles or hurt in any way," he said.

"We were not particularly worried for our own safety."

About 3000 people of a crowd estimated at 8000 remained for an hour after play was halted.

Many stood in front of the pavilion and dressing rooms, which were guarded by a thick cordon of police.

Match to re-start

The match will be re-started tomorrow, at normal playing time.

West Indian captain Alvin Kallicharran had scored a superb 126, probably the best innings from a batsman from either side during the series. He came to the wicket with the West Indies staggering at 3 for 43. They slumped further to 5 for 88, but

Kallicharran, batting immaculately, played his team back into a position to draw before he was out with 10 overs and one ball of the mandatory 20 overs in the last hour remaining.

At that stage the West Indies were 9 for 242.

Newspaper article on the riot of 1978.

First-class averages

BATTING (minimum 500 runs. * Denotes not out)

	Inns.	N.O.	H.S.	Runs	Av.	100s
Gomes (WI)	10	2	200*	712	89.0	3
Javed Miandad (Pak.)	11	2	158*	682	75.7	2
Darling (SA)	17	3	134	1011	72.3	3
McCosker (NSW)	15	3	146*	796	66.3	4
Wessels (Qld.)	18	—	220	1094	60.7	5
Ritchie (Qld.)	16	2	136*	833	59.5	3
Dyson (NSW)	14	1	127*	709	54.5	3
G. Marsh (WA)	10	—	176	545	54.5	2
Wiener (Vic.)	17	1	221*	847	52.9	3
Hughes (WA)	15	1	113	706	50.4	3
Crowe (SA)	18	4	157	704	50.2	3
Phillips (SA)	19	1	260	857	47.6	2
Kerr (SA)	14	1	158	613	47.2	3
Laird (WA)	16	2	110*	659	47.0	1
Toohey (NSW)	13	2	137	511	46.4	1
Hookes (SA)	17	1	106	703	43.9	1
Border (Qld.)	15	2	126	530	40.7	1
Wood (WA)	16	2	151	569	40.6	2
Yallop (Vic.)	18	1	111*	647	38.0	1
T. Chappell (NSW)	17	3	89	533	38.0	—

BOWLING (20 wickets, average 40 or less)

	O.	M.	Runs	Wkts.	Av.
Garner (WI)	135.3	51	372	23	16.1
Holding (WI)	214.3	49	535	32	16.7
Alderman (WA)	241	60	627	37	16.9
Stephenson (Tas.)	229.5	56	630	36	17.5
Inverarity (SA)	343.2	117	639	30	21.3
Lillee (WA)	300	75	819	37	22.1
Lawson (NSW)	200.4	48	533	24	22.2
Yardley (WA)	360.4	73	1105	49	22.5
Iqbal Qasim (Pak.)	214.4	56	532	23	23.1
Hoiland (NSW)	332.4	128	661	27	24.4
Imran Khan (Pak.)	281.2	66	686	28	24.5
Callen (Vic.)	265.1	45	789	31	25.4
Winter (SA)	318.4	97	773	28	27.6
Parkinson (SA)	310.5	75	851	28	30.3
Pascoe (NSW)	234.3	45	760	23	33.0
Sleep (SA)	343.3	96	878	26	33.7
Beard (NSW)	355	116	747	22	33.9
Hogan (Vic.)	280.3	90	735	20	36.7
Bright (Vic.)	350.1	109	742	20	37.1
Thomson (Qld)	246.1	46	788	21	37.5
Higgs (Vic.)	395.3	78	1141	29	39.3

CATCHES

WICKETKEEPERS — R. Marsh (WA), caught 37, stumped nil; Wright (SA), 30, 2; Rixon (NSW), 21, 3.

FIELDING — Serjeant (WA), 23; Laird (WA) 14; Hookes (SA) 14.

Topping the Australian Batting Average, then overlooked for the tour of Pakistan.

4TH. TEST v ENGLAND 1978-79

Standing: W.M. DARLING, G. DYMOCK, A.G. HURST, P.M. TOOHEY, B. YARDLEY (12th),
            J.D. HIGGS, A.R. BORDER.
Sitting: G.M. WOOD, J.A. MACLEAN, G.N. YALLOP (capt.), R.M. HOGG, K.J. HUGHES.

Australia v England, SCG, 1978-79.

Dressing room celebration after Test match win against Pakistan,
Perth, 1980. I was Man of the Match

A book cover with my two good mates Graeme Wood and Rodney Hogg.

Hook Shot, Australia v West Indies, Barbados, 1977

Being feld in Test Match v England, MCG, 1980.
The bowler is Bob Willis

Pull Shot v
West Indies,
SCG, 1982. Viv
Richards is in
the foreground.

14. Buckets

Georgetown, Guyana, West Indies, 1978.

Guyana is on the mainland of South America unlike the islands of the West Indies, yet it is closely linked to the Caribbean through cricket and calypso music. Muddy water from the dense rainforests is washed towards the coast by torrential tropical rain making the sea brown and murky with beaches that are muddy and uninviting. The weather is extremely hot and humid.

The region is noted for its gold products, and we all went out to buy the mandatory necklaces, bracelets, bangles, and rings. We later found out that it wasn't much cheaper than anywhere else in the world.

Georgetown is also home of the legendary West Indian player and captain Clive Lloyd. On one occasion our bus arrived at the ground surrounded by cheering, waving autograph hunters. We thought that we were royalty and puffed our chests out. Unbeknown to us, Clive had pulled up behind us in his car and was immediately surrounded by well-wishers. Our misconceived popularity left us pretty much deflated as we trudged our way to the change rooms without being stopped for one autograph.

Clive certainly deserved his elite status in the cricket world.

We were staying in a relatively modern hotel on the outskirts of Georgetown, and everything was going well for a couple of days before the electricity went off. Hence, a host of creature comforts were out including the elevators and the air conditioning. Then the water supply broke down resulting in no showers, washing clothes, or flushing toilets. We could, however, have a shower and rinse our clothes at the ground. Also, some caring locals offered showers, meals, and other necessities. It reminded me of my junior cricket days when we were billeted out.

The hotel pool wasn't available because there was no electricity to run the pumps. The smell from the toilets started to permeate the building. In desperation, the hotel management issued each room with a bucket to fill from the pool to replenish toilet cisterns. On the twelfth floor, with out-of-order lifts, it became quite a challenge to reach our rooms with any water left in the buckets that, incidentally, did not have handles. We opened all the windows to get some airflow into the rooms, but in came giant mosquitoes and the smell of rotting seaweed.

Not the best preparation for a Test match! However, if

it was it a conspiracy to wear us down it backfired. We put on a record second innings chase of 362 runs. Baz made 126, Craig (Sarge) Sargent scored 124 and Stumpa remained not out on 39. We won by 3 wickets. I didn't trouble the scorers at all.

15. 21 Today

Kingston, Jamaica, West Indies, 1978

There were always two or three days between the lead-up first-class games and Test matches. Practice was mandatory along with team meetings and other functions. My 21st birthday fell on one of the lead-up days and the boys kept me busy with practice in the morning. Then they did their best to embarrass me with a cake and speeches. We had been together for nearly three months, so each of us had something smart to say.

As the beaches around Kingston were not the best, we decided to go to the resort town of Ocho Rios about 100 kilometres away on the north coast in the Montego Bay region. We passed through a place called Spanish Town which our guide told us was notorious for its hard sell, and lawlessness. No one got off the bus. Rather, toilet stops were made in the jungle.

Ocho Rios was reminiscent of the Gold Coast at home, but with a big American influence. Lunch, beer, souvenirs and generally making a nuisance became the order of the day. We tried paragliding and water skiing until we thought about pulled muscles not being an ideal outcome before a Test match.

Soon we were back on the bus to Spanish Town. This time we had a bit more bravado, so we took a stroll to the nearest bar. It was like walking into a Wild West saloon with bat wing doors. The Reggae music stopped, and twenty West Indian Rastafarians turned and stared at us through the thick marijuana smoke haze. We nervously backed up, stumbling over each other through the bat wings to get back on the bus. Best to get the hell out of Dodge City!

Downtown Kingston was off limits to us, so more food and drinks were ordered back at the Pegasus Hotel. Thommo introduced me to a drink called the Green Lizard, a concoction of creme de menthe and brandy. It took its toll very quickly and it put a sudden end to my birthday celebrations.

Morning came with the usual grunts and groans and a few headache tablets. In recovery mode, I ran a hot bath. God knows what for, as it was hot and humid outside. Then, I was interrupted by a phone call in the bathroom. I suddenly remembered that the award-winning Adelaide breakfast radio show of Baz and Pilko had booked a call to wish me happy birthday recognising the time difference between Australia and the Windies. (In those days you had to book a phone call some days in advance to communicate with back home).

My coordination wasn't all that flash, so when I picked up the phone with my soapy hands it promptly slipped and fell into the bath. My immediate thought was about electricity (there was none of course) and I jumped out of the bath in fright. Finally, it all became a bit too much, so I just curled up on the floor cushioned by some towels with Baz and Pilko only receiving a gurgling response on the submerged phone.

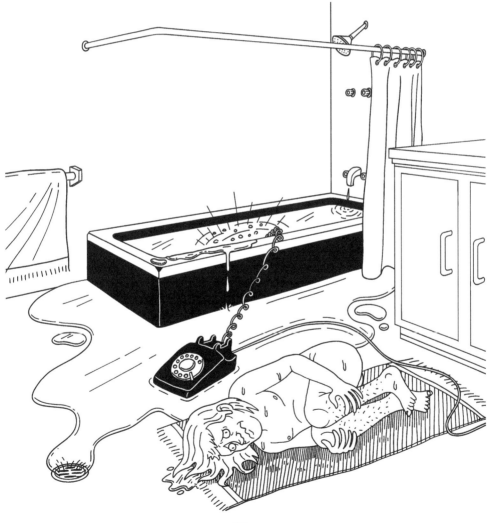

I was having a wonderful sleep when a few teammates burst into the room with a sheet and proceeded to roll me up like a chicken wrap. Next thing I was cast into the pool as they all sang happy birthday for the tenth time.

The cool water jolted my senses, and I wondered if Baz and Pilko were still on the phone. I also realised that I was still in the nude, and to a chorus of lewd comments, I wrapped the wet sheet, resembling a Toga, around me and dripped my way back to my room.

When I returned home to Adelaide, I made a point of apologising to Baz and Pilko.

16. Riot

Kingston, Jamaica, West Indies, 1978.

did not have a great playing tour of the West Indies. The final Test of the tour was at Sabina Park Cricket Ground in Jamaica. I thought I was lucky to even be named as 12th man.

It was a period of political unrest in Jamaica and the locals were ready to protest and riot at the drop of a hat. Add a mix of alcohol, drugs, heat, mounting crowd unrest, the threat of a Test defeat, and Sabina Park quickly turned into a powder keg.

On the fifth day we were in a great position to win the game, needing to take only two more wickets with 120 runs still in hand. The fuse was lit after the eighth wicket fell in controversy with the outgoing West Indian batsman questioning the decision. As 12th man, I was fielding in the covers next to Kim Hughes at cover point. A house brick came hurtling between the two of us. The first thing that went through my mind was that someone in the crowd had a pretty good arm! It turned out to be a bit more than that.

Things quickly escalated with locals throwing whatever they could find on to the ground. Rubbish was set alight on the terraces, as were dilapidated grandstands. Our captain, Bob Simpson, was cool in the crisis. He called us into a huddle around the pitch with the umpires and West Indian batsmen. Fortunately, the West Indian Cricket Board had sensed that something like this might happen so the riot police were on standby. Very quickly the police surrounded us.

The rioters then broke through the boundary fences and stormed the field. Initially, as a naïve 21-year-old, I thought this was all a bit of fun, but my reaction immediately turned to trepidation and survival. All sorts of objects were raining down upon us and each policeman had the job of protecting an individual player or umpire. They raised their shields over us like an umbrella forgoing their own safety. Tear gas drifted across the field and bullets were fired. Later reports stated the bullets were rubber. However, as a country boy who grew up with guns, I knew some of the ammunition was real.

Back in the change rooms the police had us barricaded and we hunkered down for the next two hours. Suddenly, upon instructions from security, we made a break for the team bus leaving all our gear and belongings behind. A cavalcade of police and army vehicles then escorted us

back to the hotel. Nobody in our touring party was hurt and we all remain thankful to the police and defence personnel for protecting us from this uprising.

Various officials, players and umpires received death threats during the night. Jack Anderson, a West Indian reporter, who we got to know well, was murdered in his home. This prompted the West Indian Cricket Board to abandon the game. We offered to return the next day to make for up lost time, but the Board rejected our offer. This was the first game in cricket history abandoned by a riot.

We did return to the ground the next day to get our gear, but the room had been looted badly. Some of our green baggies were stuffed down toilets and we were concerned about where the rest of our gear had gone.

As it was near the end of the tour, the West Indies Cricket Board and the Jamaican Government wanted us out of the country as quickly as possible, basically for our own safety. The ramifications of a player injured, or worse, was just too great.

Without the riot, Australia would have won the abandoned game still having ample time to take the final two West Indian wickets. This would have resulted in a more respectable 3-2 series loss on West Indian soil.

17. Scooters

Bermuda, 1978.

The mystique of the infamous Bermuda Triangle has captured people's minds for years, and I must admit being a little nervous when flying into the Triangle's invisible borders during the four-hour flight from Jamaica.

The Commonwealth country of Bermuda, with its capital of Hamilton, is in the Atlantic Ocean off the Georgia coast of the USA. It is the perfect blend of British and Caribbean cultures and is a true retreat destination for the rich and famous, predominantly from the US and the UK. The thing that you notice when flying in are the unusual pink sandy beaches that surround the coastline and the abundance of pleasure craft from the smallest of yachts, to the largest of luxury motor yachts, and the Super boats of the mega rich.

We were there to play five one-day games against the country's combined teams. It was all part of the West Indies tour, so we wanted to finish on a winning note. We won all five games, even with borrowed cricket gear after the Jamaican episode. I did well in the four games that I played and capped off what was otherwise an ordinary three months. There was, however, plenty of time for rest and recreation which was very welcome after the pressures of the Caribbean.

Scooters were primarily the main mode of transport for any visitor to the island and with no licence required, along with a dose of true Aussie competitiveness, the bravado was brought out in most of us. As with the Mini Moke in Barbados, these bikes seemed to go, or were made to go, faster, brake harder and go anywhere that they shouldn't, more than any other bike.

Of course, there were mishaps, but nothing too dramatic. Probably the most serious was Bob Simpson (Simmo) coming to terms with a rough road and skidding along on his behind to a painful stop. The resulting gravel rash was bad enough for him to eventually be taken to hospital for a good clean up. It made for many sleepless nights for Simmo, lying on his stomach, and a very uncomfortable plane trip home. I don't think that he would have ridden another bike of any description wearing bathers again! Ian Callen (Mad Dog) and I were keen on riding up some hotel stairs, for no reason at all. Going up was easy but coming down was a bit of a challenge. I was savvy enough to use only my back brake, while Mad Dog used his front brake and soon found himself at the bottom of the stairs, well before the

bike got there. The wash up from that was a retrieval truck and $350 in damages. Not to be deterred, Mad Dog promptly got another scooter.

Having had a bit of a chuckle at most of my teammates' minor mishaps, and thinking that I was left unscathed, I then had a little altercation with a rock pool in an area that was off limits. Served me right. I managed to lose a big toenail and gained an exhaust pipe burn. As with Simmo, a few sleepless nights followed.

It was such a good bonding time, even the endless official functions were enjoyable and the invitations to mix with the upper echelon in their homes, or on their pleasure crafts were not to be passed up.

Towards the end of this ideal time, players started to drift home as flights became available. Mad Dog and I decided to spend ten days touring around the UK. Two days later, Mad Dog was found wading across a frigid stream and ascending a Scottish hill with a plastic bag trying to collect a small patch of snow. It was to be ice for an Esky! That's another story.

I was lucky enough to return to Bermuda, with my wife Tania, in 2006 to play in a T20 Seniors competition for Australia. The culture, the people, and the laid-back lifestyle hadn't changed. More importantly, the lack of commercial development was refreshing. It's the way the law makers of the island had intended it to be and is all for the better.

18. Her Majesty

Buckingham Palace, London, 1979.

Travelling to England on a cricket tour involves a lot of pomp and ceremony. There was none bigger than meeting the Queen at Buckingham Palace for the World Cup tour.

We were all resplendent in our team blazers with shoes polished and hair neatly trimmed. Some of us had our green and gold ties in our pockets because the weather was warm, yet we intended to put them on before being introduced to Her Majesty.

The bus drove past the Grenadier Guards and through the ornate front gates with wheels crunching the gravel of the driveway and courtyard. Initially, I was not greatly impressed with the palace, but we then entered grand corridors to the reception hall surrounded by gilded picture frames of landscapes and portraits, some from floor to ceiling, along with fascinating ceremonial gifts from all over the world. It was mesmerising. The boy from Ramco stood in amazement.

In the waiting hall we gathered with other World Cup cricket teams, and it became a little stuffy. Some players were loosening their ties, while others were putting them on. Tie I thought, checking my pocket. Not there! Shit, I thought, it must have fallen out of my pocket in the bus. As a 21-year-old, organisation was not a priority, and my country fashions did not include ties. Meeting royalty without a tie was just not the done thing. But it was too late to do anything about it as we were starting to file in to meet the Queen. I ducked out of sight from our team manager, David Richards, and captain Kim Hughes, and waited for something miraculous to happen.

An announcer said, "Introducing the Australian team." I shuffled to the back of the line hoping not to be noticed. I secured my top button to make it look as though I had made an effort and then out of the corner of my eye, I noticed the green ties of the Pakistan team. They were a darker green than ours, but green all the same. I quickly raced over and pleaded my case with one of the Pakistani players. The idea was to quickly borrow his tie and then return it to him after meeting the Queen and Princess Anne. Thankfully, I appeared sufficiently desperate and stood there to meet the Royals in my Pakistan tie with just a minute to spare.

A bow of the head and a not too soft, nor too hard, handshake and it was quickly over. David and Kim had their eyes on me right from the start. No wonder they

both had a nervous smile when introducing me to Her Majesty ushering her on quickly. I later found out they had noticed I was wearing the Pakistan tie, yet had the good grace not to mention it.

I thought the day couldn't get any worse until the team photos were about to be taken in front of the palace. I then had to go through the whole process again to borrow a tie.

Obviously, it was a great honour, and I was proud to be part of it, as was my father would have been when he met Queen Elizabeth twenty-five years earlier. He was representing the South Australian Country XI against England at Adelaide Oval in 1954.

I did return to Buckingham Palace with my wife, Tania, in 1986 to attend a garden party which the Queen held on various occasions throughout the summer. I felt resplendent in my morning suit, top hat, salmon tie and gloves, while Tania was elegantly dressed in a pink and white dress and coat, hat and, of course the mandatory gloves. Jewellery had to be conservative and kept at a minimum. That turned a few heads on the top deck of a London bus before arriving at the Palace.

We did manage to be seated next to the Chancellor of Oxford University, an interesting fellow, and while Tania was quite at home when discussing academia, I was distracted by the gardens and landscaping, and was looking in hope for a like-minded person, much like when I was at school. During the afternoon I did find it a bit unsettling to have an attendant, who's command of the English language was impeccable, brush down the back of my ensemble while I was standing at the urinal. It would have been ungentlemanly of me to protest. It was a very hot day in London, and the same attendant, with a damp towel wiped the inner lining of my top hat. I needed another gin and tonic after that episode.

Looking back on the World Cup tour I did have a similar lavatory episode. The tour offered plenty of free time so Kevin Wright, Andrew Hilditch, Graeme Porter and I set off across the channel to Paris. Upon using the facilities, and being catered for by an attendant, I walked out with a skip in my step only to be hunted down by a snarling Alsatian with fangs bared. I thought I would make a run for it but thought better of it as the mood of the dog hadn't changed. The dog belonged to the attendant and (unbeknown to me) was made to set upon any user that had not paid. To the amusement of my teammates a franc or two was paid and a much more placid Alsatian nestled back on his dog bed.

19. Paddy Wagon

Hindley Street, Adelaide, 1980.

Whenever I reminisce about my playing days, Hookesy features strongly in many of my on and off-field experiences. After all, you can't play and be friends with a person for a fair part of your life without having some stories to tell.

There were many fun times, one of which saw the two of us messing around in Hindley Street one night after a win. It was late when out of the blue a police paddy wagon screeched to a halt in front of us. Surely we hadn't created that much trouble we thought! "You blokes, with blonde hair," one of the officers said. (Hookesy loved it when people thought he had blonde hair. Most people couldn't see it though). "Do you want to be in a line-up back at headquarters? There's been an assault down the street."

Well, that was like a red rag to a bull, and we were in that paddy wagon in a flash thinking this could be a bit of fun. At police headquarters we were unceremoniously jostled into a room with the typical height scale on the back wall and the big one-way glass in front of us. I then started to get a little nervous worrying the witness might get it wrong.

Hookesy was cool and confident as usual. One of the policemen recognised him and, of course, Hookesy started up a conversation with him. This eased our nerves greatly. After a few minutes each person in the line-up was asked to leave the room except suspect Number 5. Moments later the perpetrator (Number 5) was put in handcuffs.

Still in playful mood, Hooksey gave me a little nudge as we walked past the fingerprint desk. Overbalancing, I found myself sprawled over a neatly laid out desk. Ink, pads, papers, and other paraphernalia ended up on the floor along with me.

The other blokes in the line-up all had a good old laugh, as did Hookesy, although he looked a little sheepish. A stern looking policeman said that it was time for us to get out, but not before Hooksey smoothed things over with a few autographs.

Hookesy and I ended up back in Hindley Street and continued on with the festivities, albeit with fingerprint ink all over my white body shirt, cherry red flares, white belt and platform shoes. More importantly my long blonde mullet wasn't tusselled. What a great look that was!

A few years later, Merv Kowald, a teammate at Salisbury, was the assigned police officer attending a fracas in Hindley Street in which someone put a kink

in my nose, or maybe have straightened it. Two of my friends at the time were Anthony Handrickan, a fellow South Australian opening batsman, and Mick Brien, a first-class umpire. Neither of them showed much concern for my injury as the sun came up over Hindley Street. Merv, however, with a big smile on his face, escorted me to hospital knowing full well that I would have been making a nuisance of myself.

20. Fireworks

Kanpur, India, 1980.

Kanpur is in northeastern India about 500 kilometres from New Delhi. It was the first time a Test had been played in the city, so the interest in the game, and the Australian team, was unprecedented. About 20,000 people came to watch us practise on the day before the game started. One little boy, about ten years old, with only one leg, got some special attention having a bat in the nets, much to the crowd's delight.

I remember getting a few runs in this game, which was marred by an unusual incident. Over the mid-off boundary, deep in the crowd, was a person with a mirror. Each time I faced up to the bowler on his approach, the mirror was deliberately flashed in my eyes. Naturally, I had to pull away time and time again. Unbeknown to the offender in the throng, his persistence was pinpointing his exact location to local police. Newspaper reports next day said that he was banished from the ground with no fine, but with one broken arm. As an aside, I read that

Joe Darling's teams many years earlier also had trouble with spectators and mirrors in England.

In the Kanpur Test, I managed to misjudge a bouncing ball while fielding and required five stitches in my eyelid.

From there it was an overnight train journey to New Delhi in the so-called sleeper class, which consisted of a padded blanket rolled out on a wooden bench. It was quite claustrophobic, complete with creepy crawlies. There wasn't a lot to do in our down time in India, particularly on a night train, so reading was big. Wilbur Smith novels were the favourite, and it was my job to source these novels, and in sequence. I am still engrossed in Wilbur's novels to this day.

It was a practical joke of mine to pass these novels on to the next keen reader, but beforehand I would tear ten or so pages from the back of the book and keep them in a safe spot. These pages were normally the uncertain climax of Wilbur's novels. The reader was kept in suspense and needed these pages like a drug. This came to a head on the train and the unsuspecting reader was Rodney (Hoggy) Hogg. Holding them fluttering by an open window, I said, "Hoggy, are you looking for these?"

Unbeknown to Hoggy, they were pages from another, unrelated, book. I let the bogus pages blow out the window into the night. Hoggy stared in disbelief before springing into action to inflict a bit of corporal punishment. I then came clean with the original rightful pages handing them to him. He admitted I'd tricked him good and proper. Nobody seemed to learn from these episodes as I would catch others time and time again.

Hoggy and I worked and played together for a long time. He was and still is a good mate. Along with Lillee and Thomson he was revered by all the world's best batsmen of that era.

We pulled into New Delhi at dawn. Even at such an early hour, the roads were packed with a cacophony of busy city noises. I am sure that obtaining a drivers licence in India includes a requirement to constantly beep the car horn.

I knew some day my teammates would pay me back for the practical jokes on the train, and I didn't have to wait long. During the Test in New Delhi there was the usual line up for toilets in the change rooms. I found a cubical with a toilet bowl as a urinal was not going to suffice. With most of my teammates milling around and whispering, I should have sensed that some shenanigans were going to happen. It was then that Alan (AB) Border rolled a fireworks cracker under the cubicle door. If the 'Delhi Belly' didn't loosen things up, the cracker certainly did!

Even before the sparks went out, I was thinking of payback. Let the games begin! My full-sized rubber Cobra made its debut soon after the toilet incident. Something about AB and his bed comes to mind.

Fireworks in India were easy to come by, and they

were used for all sorts of entertainment, particularly by fans at the grounds. For some in the crowd it was a laugh, while for others perhaps a move to unsettle touring teams. Anyone fielding within cracker throwing range was fair game. Needless to say, fieldsmen were shell-shocked by the end of the day. Nobody wanted to field in the outer.

Another fan favourite was throwing food onto the field. This would encourage the hawk-like Kites to swoop for the food and the players. Add the horrendous heat, smoke, dust and crackers, and Test cricket in India was quite draining. On our tour, there were reports of darts being found in the turf. I saw no evidence of this, but perhaps it was a ploy from the Indian press to rattle our nerves even more.

Crackers were used by us, in more ways than one. Apart from the Alan Border type tomfoolery, they were used as a scare tactic against wild dogs in Bangalore. These wild dog dogs would drift in after dark from the nearby bush lands and shanty towns where they would camp under our stand-alone units that surrounded the hotel complex. They would bark and growl at any passers-by which spawned a myriad of practical jokes amongst the players. It was no joke, however, when we learnt to arm ourselves with a cricket bat and crackers to ward off these scavengers. No-one ever got bitten but it certainly sharpened one's senses when moving around the grounds.

So much for occupational health and safety back then.

21. *"Got to go Baz."*

Bombay, India, 1980.

You don't have to wait long in India before contracting the notorious Delhi Belly. No matter how careful you are about hygiene, the bug will still prevail, multiple times and from a myriad of sources. We all got it, and at its worst, it was hard to even lift your head off a pillow. Playing with Delhi Belly was literally an art form!

On one occasion 'Baz' Wood and I were rooming together with a simultaneous dose. No amount of pills, potions, snake oils or local remedies would work, so we just had to let it pass. And pass it did! Baz had the vomiting version while I had the diarrhoea variety. We were both up one night with stomach cramps so there was a constant race for the bathroom space. Baz got there first and had his head in the toilet. This put me in a difficult spot. The shower recess was full of freshly washed clothes, so the last resort was the hand basin. In desperation, I warned Baz to move his toothbrush and comb, but it was too late!

We were both physically and mentally fatigued, but still mustered the energy for a good laugh. I did my best to clean things up. I'm sure the cleaner wasn't all that happy the next day, but I did leave her 200 rupees for her trouble. Needless to say, I bought Baz some new toiletries, but made him wait a day or two.

When ill with Delhi Belly we were not allowed to travel on the team bus for the risk of spreading the bug, so taxis were arranged on a daily basis. Generally, two or three of us would be feeling poorly, so we got to know the Indian taxi drivers well. The Tuk Tuk cabs, fashioned from three-wheeled motorbikes, were better if you had a vomiting attack.

On a happier note, we always tried to have a friendly chat with the drivers. We'd ask each driver if he played cricket and whether he was a batsman or bowler. Invariably, the reply would be, "No sir, I am an all-rounder!" We'd lay bets on getting this response and it was always good fun. The same game can be played with taxi drivers in Australia today.

Before going to India, I weighed 79 kilograms. When I returned, I was 11 kilograms lighter. I have been asked many times what India is really like. My response is quite direct, "One of the best things about coming home from a Test tour of India is that you can fart with confidence!"

Having said that, India is a fascinating place with its rich history and culture. I had some wonderful experiences in that country and would love to return to discover more. The food, customs, landscapes and general hustle and bustle make it fascinating. The people are amazing, and overall, India is a true wonder of the world.

22. Fly Home

Melbourne Cricket Ground. 1982.

For a cricketer, there is nothing better than playing against the West Indies at the MCG on a hot Melbourne day with 80,000 fans looking on.

The day before our One Day International, I was relaxing in the pool when I noticed a rash on my stomach. I wasn't too concerned thinking it was only a sweat rash from the morning's net and fielding practice. That night I was a bit restless with the itching and the heat emanating from the rash, which was quickly developing into welts.

Next morning at the ground, the doctor on duty suggested it was an allergic reaction, so he filled me up with antihistamines. Cold showers were also recommended.

We were fielding first, and as the heat rose, so did my discomfort. Our captain, Greg Chappell, let me off the ground to cool down and get further treatment. I was on a bench in the change room with a wet towel over me when a nameless official/selector came in and gave me the stare. It was a look as if to say, "Get the hell back out there!" I did return to the field, but as I found out later, the damage had been done and a decision was made.

In the change rooms after the game, we were milling around with luminaries including Dennis Lillee, Rod Marsh, Jeff Thomson, Allan Border and Doug Walters while waiting for our tickets to be handed out for the flight to Sydney, where we were to play the next one dayer. Everyone got a ticket except me, so I naturally asked for mine. The manager then handed me my ticket from Melbourne to Adelaide, not Melbourne to Sydney. This meant I was flying home and had been dropped from the team. No explanation, nothing but a plane ticket. It was pretty gutless. At least one of the selectors could have shown some common courtesy. But I supposed that when treated to all the food and drink throughout the day, they just didn't have time to offer me an explanation.

My teammates showed their support for me, and disbelief in the way it had been handled. It was an unforgettable show of friendship, and to have Doug Walters in that group of supporters softened the blow for me considerably. Doug was my favourite player when I was a kid, and it was now a real honour to be playing with him. Featuring in a sixty-run partnership with Doug against Pakistan on the SCG was one of my greatest experiences.

I never played for Australia again. Back in Adelaide I was diagnosed with shingles.

Apart from the one-day series, I was overlooked for

the forthcoming Test tour to Pakistan after scoring 1,011 first-class runs at a season average of 72. Again, there was no explanation given.

Some years earlier, a journalist at Melbourne airport told me I had been dropped from the Australian team and the media suggested I was a scapegoat for the poor performance of the side. There had been no contact from a selector or official.

One would hope that communications and basic decency among the decision-makers have improved, particularly as the support staff for the current Australian team is 15. When I played, we only had the manager.

23. Short Cut

Adelaide Oval, 1983.

n first-class cricket in the early 1980s, there was a big push on physical fitness. Gym work, running, cross training, and whatever made you sweat and puff hard became the norm. While most of us enjoyed this aspect of our match preparation, some started to suggest the preoccupation with physical exercise came at a cost by foregoing precious time practising core skills of batting, bowling, and fielding.

South Australia's coach around this time was Howard (Chops) Mutton, a schoolteacher who loved sport and physical fitness. He was in his early 60s and enjoyed being with the team, running alongside us and generally being our 'go to' man. I'm not sure whether the extra training made us better cricketers, but the competitive aspect of it helped build camaraderie and team spirit.

I remember one Sunday morning before a trial game when Chops had entered us all in the City to Bay Fun Run of about 12 kilometres from Adelaide to Glenelg. We

then had to find our way back to Adelaide No. 2 Oval to play a trial game despite some aches and pains from the so-called fun run. Each of the players felt it was ridiculous as none of us would be at our best to impress the selectors. I remember Hoggy fronting Chops to express his displeasure declaring, "It would have been more beneficial to practise our skills rather than training for the Olympics." However, we all played and made it through the day.

Sam (Parky) Parkinson is well known in Adelaide and beyond. Parky was our left arm fast bowler for many years taking over 100 first class wickets, and he was an integral member of the victorious Sheffield Shield team in 1981-1982. Parky was, and still is, an easy recruit when it comes to having a good time. Most practice nights, Chops instructed us to go on a 5.5 kilometre run around both sides of the River Torrens alongside Adelaide Oval. Invariably, Sam and I would be trudging along at the back of the pack. There were three bridges across the river that could be used as a shortcut. Depending on how we felt, Parky and I would cross one of these bridges and hide in the reeds until the last runner had passed. We'd then splash water from the river under our arms, hair, and face to simulate sweat and sprint to the oval finishing amongst the pack pretending that we were exhausted.

Nobody questioned our little escapades. However,

Chops often gave us a wry smile and a shake of his head. Without a doubt, he was on to us.

Chops died in 1992.

24. Slippery Fellow

Claypans, South Australia, 1984.

J eff (Chopper) Crowe was a New Zealand top order batsman who played for South Australia before returning home to eventually captain the Test side. On one occasion Chopper and I were invited to play in a double wicket competition at an area known as Claypans in the Lower Murray region of South Australia.

These competitions were very popular in the 1970s and 1980s, as they were run primarily to raise money for clubs and charities. Another South Australian player and good friend of mine, Peter (Sounda) Sleep, was also involved in these games.

The format was that each pair would bat for four overs and then bowl two overs each at an opposing pair. The winning pair would progress to the next round, and the loser would play-off in the Consolation Plate. The crowd parked around the ground, and of course, the bar patrons saw some big hitting from the broad-shouldered New Zealander.

At one point, play was halted as a 1.5 metre brown

snake made a pitch inspection from wicket to wicket. It obviously liked the warmth of the concrete pitch, sunning there for about five minutes, before it was ushered along with a few gentle prods from a cricket bat. Country cricket at its best. Sounda and his local partner, only known as Juggsie, won the day.

Chopper loved telling a joke. With his audience gathered under the club room awning, Chopper embarked on his delivery. He said, "Buccaneers were notorious in the 17th century for marauding Spanish ships and settlements in the Caribbean. During one dark and stormy night, Blue Beard, in the heat of battle with cannons booming and muskets popping, was worried that his Buccaneers had jumped ship. Blue Beard said to his lieutenant above the battle scuffles, din and howling wind, 'Where are your Buccaneers lieutenant, to which the lieutenant replied, **'On my *Buccan* head sir.**" On that fine note we left for Adelaide.

The hospitality of the locals was second to none with a barbecue and beer following play. The snake, on the other hand, enjoyed no such hospitality. Leaving the ground, we found it hanging on a gatepost. Apparently, a local kelpie took a liking to it.

Arriving back in Adelaide, we managed to entertain ourselves at various venues gaining access despite still wearing in our cricket clothes.

Years later, I caught up with Chopper at Trent Bridge in England where New Zealand was playing a Test match.

He introduced me to the team including the acclaimed fast bowler, Sir Richard Hadlee. This meeting led me to being invited to play in Richard's benefit game in the city of Blackpool. He and Chopper made me feel more than welcome.

Chopper now lives in Florida, and he is an International Cricket Council referee.

25. Barramundi and Crocs

Darwin, Northern Territory, 1984.

D uring my playing career, I always looked forward to the end of the season to recuperate and invariably headed for the bush to do the things I loved. I often considered playing cricket in the leagues in England but found time away from the game was more valuable for me. However, I did receive an offer from Roger Sweet, a team-mate of mine at West Torrens, and captain of the Nightcliff Cricket Club in Darwin, to play after season's end 'down the track', as the locals called any place south of Darwin.

So, off I went on this adventure leaving my fiancée, Tania, in Adelaide. Playing in Darwin provided the opportunity to try some different outdoor pursuits. The guys at the Nightcliff Cricket Club always had something going on and on one occasion we hitched a ride on an old DC3 propeller plane carrying goods between Darwin and the Tiwi Islands of Bathurst and Melville in the Timor Sea. The dents and the rust on the old bird indicated that it may have made a few covert missions in its time.

There were four of us teammates aboard along with Tony Barratt, a likeable villain as our leader, who set up a barramundi fishing trip for a couple of days. We stayed in his cabin at the aptly named Snake Bay on the north coast of Melville Island. It was an ideal tropical setting, complete with crocodiles, snakes, and mosquitoes.

A morning's coaching in the local community convinced me that cricket wasn't high on their sporting preferences and kicking a footy around was a more favoured option. After all, the Tiwi Islands are noted for producing some brilliant AFL footballers.

By lunchtime, we had the dingy floating in the backwaters of Melville Island. Most of my fishing experience was on the Murray River, where it was very hit or miss. Barramundi angling, I was told, was going to be a breeze and within two minutes I had one on the line.

I was curious about the old Lee Enfield .303 rifle strategically mounted inside the boat. What's more it was loaded! The owner of the gun (registration and licence doubtful) could see that I was itching for a shot at the abundant feral pigs. So off I went for a stalk. I was so focused on a group of four or five ferals that I completely forgot where I was and found myself up to my knees in water.

I was about fifty metres away from the boat when Tony yelled out, "Croc!" Immediately, I bolted for the boat having checked the safety catch of the .303. I reached the security of the boat in record time losing one of my

runners on the way. It was all a set up by the lads, and they all had a good laugh while I was puffing, sweating, and shaking with fear. That was the end of my hunting expedition without even firing a shot. Even though it was a 'cry wolf' event by my mates, I did learn a lesson and often think, "what if?" I kept all parts of my body in the boat from then on.

The filleting of the barramundi and the shelling of the crabs took place on the riverbank. As the Eskys were being emptied of beer, they were filled with the fillets. Surprisingly, some succulent crocodile fillets also found their way into an Esky. Perhaps a shot had been fired!

Back on the sandy beach in front of the cabin, a scene reminiscent of the *Gilligan's Island* television sitcom set, a barbecue of barramundi, crabs and croc seasoned with rosemary, a hint of garlic, and some other delicious condiments, was just the ticket. The .303 was never too far away!

Darwin provided me with many fantastic memories. Maybe in another life I would be happy to call it home.

26. Lost in Lancashire

Whalley, Lancashire, UK. 1986.

Playing in the Lancashire League is something that I should have done early in my career rather than leaving it to the end. While nowhere near the level of first-class cricket in Australia, Lancashire League provides a valuable learning and experimental platform, particularly for young cricketers.

Being the professional for the Whalley Cricket Club in Northern Lancashire came with a lot of expectation. Put simply, this expectation was that the club would win the championship. Which we did!

I found the experience of playing two, three and sometimes four times a week rewarding because if you were out of form, it wasn't long before you were back in touch. If in form, you could experiment with creative shots and work on weaker ones. As the professional at Whalley Cricket Club I had to bowl as well as bat. A simple medium pace on the grassy, wet wickets reaped many rewards. This bowling experience helped me to bowl for Kensington on the odd occasion when I returned to Adelaide.

The end-of-season trip in England was unforgettable. A bus ride to Preston, where the nightlife was the best around, was the usual destination. The bus was scheduled to leave Preston strictly at 1.00am for the trip home. Those who were late missed out. Of course, my mate John (Whitey) White and I missed the bus. Whitey was from a tiny neighbouring village to Whalley called Sabden, which is famous for its history of witchcraft through the ages.

The dilemma for Whitey and me was whether to stay in Preston or try to get home another way. I don't know what we were thinking, as home was about a thirty-minute bus ride away, but off we walked regardless. The plan was to hitch a ride from anybody heading in the general direction of home, which did happen for part of the way. However, after walking for about two hours, telling jokes, and singing songs through country hamlets and narrow laneways we'd had enough. It was getting eerily quiet, and my mind was wondering when I started thinking of the thriller book and movie, *The Hound of the Baskervilles.* I mentioned this to Whitey, and with his consciousness of witchcraft, things got a little spooky. From then on, every owl hoot and every little leaf rustle quickened our gait.

We soon spotted an outbuilding on the edge of a field that was obviously a horse stable. Being a warm night, the horses were out in the field. It didn't take too much time to have a look, kick a bit of hay around and throw a horse

blanket over us. By then it was 4.00am. With sunrise at 6.30am and after a 'swaggies breakfast' (a piss and a look around) we set off on our hike hoping for a ride but ended up doing lots more walking. We were in no rush, so we had a proper breakfast, morning tea and lunch in villages along the way.

Smelling like Phar Lap, and with straw in our hair, we arrived back at the club about 3 o'clock in the afternoon. Some of the younger lads were still kicking on from the previous night and were intrigued with our adventure, but at the same time not at all interested in our welfare. Upon retrieving my car keys, I realised that the flat keys where I was living in Great Harwood with my wife, Tania, were on the key ring. When the flat door was locked on the outside, nobody could get in or out! Tania had been locked in a small flat above a butcher's shop for 30 hours with no phone of any description. There was silence at home for a few days after that.

It was a long and tough ordeal with Whitey, but a lifelong friend was made. If it wasn't for him, I could still be roaming aimlessly around Lancashire.

Two other Aussie cricketers, John 'Moose' McGuire and Brendan 'Bushy' McArdle, were living in Great Harwood, about 5km from Whalley, at the same time. John played many years for Queensland and in a few Test matches, while Brendon played for Victoria as an all-rounder. I spent many fun hours playing with and against them. Many other Aussies were playing in the Northern Leagues, so there was plenty of interaction, mainly about the football back home.

Ironically, three years earlier, John hit me in the eye while bowling in a Sheffield Shield game. A week in hospital, and the rest of the season off, was the result. I still have problems with that eye not adjusting to the light as it should, but certainly don't hold a grudge towards John.

However, when a fast bowler says that he doesn't bowl to deliberately hit or hurt a batsman, I suggest his integrity must come into question. Jeff Thomson openly admitted this during an interview in his tear-away days. Thommo's honesty has always been refreshing.

There have been many times while batting that a fast bowler has openly said, "I am f.....g going to kill you." (Certainly, a death threat in my book). It used to infuriate me that on these occasions that if I (or any batsman) retaliated against this attack, it was I who got reprimanded by the umpire. There was a fast bowler from New South Wales that used to threaten me on regular occasions. My response would be a variation of words to the effect of, " If you hit me, you better make sure I stay down, because if I get up I will shove this bat up your arse, sideways." The umpires didn't like this sort of talk. Seriously, after a death threat, come on!

I was never quite the same after being struck in the eye. I kept playing for South Australia for a few seasons which led to a few more knocks in the head. These head injuries resulted, later in life, a condition known as Post Traumatic Epilepsy. I really didn't want to be there for those last couple of seasons and should have retired much earlier.

27. Saint David's

Llandudno, Wales, 1986.

While playing as a professional in Lancashire, part of my contract was to travel to, and coach at, Saint David's College in the Welsh seaside town of Llandudno. It was about a two-hour drive from Great Harwood. Tania and I would travel on a Sunday night and spend two nights in a quaint little seaside hotel in Llandudno. We would then return to Lancashire two days later to our rudimentary lodgings in a one room flat with a well-used couch and a single mattress on the floor as the sleeping arrangements. It was always frosty in the flat as it was perched on top of a butcher's freezer. It had the added luxury of an outdoor toilet.

Saint David's College was set on vast, green grounds with panoramic views of the coastal hills and Irish Sea. A beautiful old English manor was used as the administration and staff areas. The headmaster, Mr Mayor, also resided in this manor and we were invited to dinner with him and others every Monday evening. Nobody knew his first name, so it was always Mr Mayor. He was always the epitome of upper-class Welsh gentry with his silk smoking jacket coupled with a matching cravat. His jet-black hair was always anointed with some exotic tonic. Being very generous, Mr Mayor's pre-dinner sherries and post-dinner ports and cigars around the fireplace were memorable.

The coaching was great, and the school won all five games when I was coach. However, I think they were pretty much unbeatable well before I arrived. The breaks during play and practice sessions were great because I could meet college staff members from all parts of the world and there was one very memorable occasion.

One of the groundsmen, Tomos (a good, strong Welsh name), cut his hand during an altercation with a lawn mower. After stitching, he was put on light duties and spent far too much time in the staff room playfully annoying the staff. I had made good friends with a Dutch ex-pat called Johan. On this occasion, my Dutch friend was stirring his tea ready to sit down when I called out to him across the room, "How is Johan?" Tomos, who was sitting next to Johan, thought I had asked him, "How is your hand?" Sounding very much like, "How is Johan?", Tomos responded by raising his bandaged hand saying, ***"Not bad. I get the stitches out next week."*** The room erupted into laughter with dropped scones and spilled tea. Meanwhile, Tomos crawled under a rug!

28. No Payment Accepted

Bogor, Indonesia, 2008.

have been fortunate over the years to do some coaching in countries where cricket was becoming increasingly popular. I've been a guest coach in Malaysia, Singapore, and Indonesia where my role was to develop players at all levels. I have no doubt that if funding and on-going coaching expertise is forthcoming these countries will, in time, compete at the higher levels of world cricket.

Bogor is a city about 30 kilometres from Jakarta, but the focus of this story is on a small village to the south where a very special display of hospitality and helpfulness presented itself.

When I arrived in Bogor, I quickly made friends with an expat New Zealander named Alex, who helped run the coaching program in the area. We shared an interest in motorbikes and Alex said I could borrow one to go exploring around the countryside. Inspecting the 175cc Yamaha, I knew I wasn't going to get very far. It was old, battered, and held together by flaking rust.

Everyone in Indonesia seemed to ride a scooter or motorbike and it is an acquired skill in the local conditions. To have a whole family perched on, or hanging off a bike, was not uncommon. Tania would have been horrified about the adventure that I was about to embark on, but with travel insurance I felt bullet proof. Reading the fine print on the insurance certificate later revealed some exclusions!

Off I set with no helmet. A pair of shorts, T-shirt and runners comprised my only personal protective equipment. I started to loosen up on leaving the hustle and pollution of the city travelling through the countryside and small villages only about five to ten kilometres apart.

The Yamaha started to struggle in the heat of the day, and coupled with its other obvious flaws, it gave one last cough before I freewheeled to a halt. Start stop, start stop were the immediate symptoms for diagnosis. Fuel OK, spark OK! What else? Probably dirty fuel. Whatever it was, I needed help to get to the nearest village where motorbike repair shops seemed to be everywhere. Hundreds of bikes and riders passed, and one eventually stopped to help. A rope on the back of his bike led me to believe that he had towed bikes before and, although quite unsettling, I was happy for his assistance. He dropped me at the first repair shop that we came to, and he was then away in a cloud of blue two stroke smoke.

No payment accepted.

A young man by the name of Daksa limped up to inquire about the problem with my motorbike. He struggled with English, but with plenty of sign language and head nodding there was hope of repair. A flush of the fuel filter and a half a cup of methylated spirits along with a few full throttle laps of the village square fixed the problem, apparently because of water and dirt in the fuel.

No payment accepted.

When Daksa discovered I was Australian he showed me through to the back of the shop to a living area to meet his family and to welcome me for their midday meal. Despite the communication difficulties, I spent the next hour eating and chatting. I have always been a steak and chips person, but the steamed chicken, rice and spices with Daksa's family were superb.

Waiting for the heat of the day to subside, Daksa and I fossicked around his workshop, where I tinkered and learnt more about the mechanics of motorbikes.

No payment accepted.

Riding back to the hotel, I thought about the great day that I had just had. Thinking deeper, I realised that no one on Earth had known where I had been on this day. No passport, not much money, no licence, no ID. Scary.

Priceless!

29. R&R

Abu Dhabi,
United Arab Emirates, 2019.

When you get the opportunity to travel Business Class and be accommodated in a six-star luxury hotel, you would very rarely pass it up. What followed were five days of rest and recreation in Abu Dhabi, with a morning of junior coaching followed by an exhibition 40/40 game between the Australian Seniors and England.

Golf was one of the options for Day One. Not being much of a golfer I volunteered to man a golf cart with Stan Gilchrist, a real good bloke who never advertised that the fact that he was the father of Adam Gilchrist. The cart was the supply line for spare equipment and refreshments of all sorts. Wayne Phillips, who is quite an accomplished golfer, won the day. However, with an empty beer Esky, the tallies on the score cards were all a bit dubious. Having an interest in horticulture I asked the head greenkeeper, how he created the greenery and lakes in a sandy desert. The answer was, "Desalination, the whole city relies on it, and is the sole reason for the massive development in recent years."

Two free days followed the arduous day of golf, so we lounged around the pool with other cricketers and guests from all over the globe. Also, during this time, shopping and sightseeing were organised for those interested in something a little livelier. I linked up with Mike Valletta from Western Australia, who has represented both Western Australia and Australia at Test level. He is also the brother-in-law of my good friend Graeme Wood. Mike and I hired a driver to show us the tourist spots, of which there weren't many, as most of the Central Business District revolved around commerce. The mega shopping centres offered all the attractions, but we wanted something a bit more cultural. We then found ourselves in the old city amongst the markets and took the opportunity to load up on exotic fruit and trinkets. A toilet was then needed, and we were pointed in the direction of a stone, stand-alone building, which seemed to be out in the desert about 200 metres away. So off we trekked.

I handed my bags to Mike so I could go in without them. There were the typical stalls on the left and a urinal on the right. The urinal was a long, raised, metal trough about seven metres long with water taps spaced evenly along the trough. I thought this was a bit weird, but I had things to do.

So, there I was whistling merrily away when I noticed to my right a local washing his face and another washing his feet from the taps, as my urine was streaming down the trough beneath them. One of them, to his credit, knew that I was an ignorant, or arrogant, foreigner and sternly pointed to the stalls. Thus, I belatedly realised that urinals did not exist in this toilet block. Another piece of culture absorbed.

Quickly I saw an opportunity to set Mike up. As we exchanged shopping bags, I told him that he MUST go to the trough on his right when he went in, as the stalls on the left were only change rooms. In he went and fronted up to the trough. Seconds later he appeared back from the block, still doing up his fly, and being ushered out by three locals who were remonstrating in some Persian dialect that we didn't comprehend. We did, however, have no trouble in understanding some universal words and the meaning of some of the hand gestures, so we thought it was time to speedily depart. I was in hysterics and Mike, after being caught short, was still in need!

The markets in the shimmering heat seemed a long way off, so we quickened our steps in pursuit of another toilet and relative safety. There, Mike who was very much more learned in the tastes of Persian cuisine, bought me a lightly spiced lentil and chickpea dish. I thought his lack of eye contact was a bit strange but thought nothing of it, until about three minutes later. The legume dish was wonderful, so I gulped it down like I had ten seconds to live, "Great!" I said as the beads of sweat started to ooze from my pores and my throat erupted in molten lava. It was hotter than the hottest vindaloo! It was then his turn to be in hysterics.

The next morning was junior coaching, and when the game started it was 44 degrees with high humidity. The sweat would drip off the end of your fingers while just standing there. Not that it bothered me, as I fielded in the shade of the grandstand and was out LBW from the first ball of our innings. Australia lost quite easily. Ian Bell and other English County players made it quite a one-sided affair.

A Bedouin Camp later that night, way out in the sand dunes, was a highlight, albeit very touristy. Here we partook of traditional dance, sampled food and drink, and of course smoked the Sheesha pipes. I must admit that it was good to get back to the hotel for a Club Sandwich with chips and a cold Diet Coke later.

This trip to Abu Dhabi will probably be my last cricket trip in a Seniors team. But never say never!

30. A Tribute

Ramco/Waikerie, South Australia, 1922-1996.

My father, Max (Diddle) Darling was my only coach as a kid. Coaching, up to and including first class cricket, was non-existent. What you learnt as a kid was it! I thank Dad for his patience and knowledge in my early years.

Dad, in short, didn't want me to take over the family property. He wanted something different, so he built me a cricket net. We must have spent thousands of hours in that rusting net among the prickles and ants where his coaching was based on a good defence. He would say that all attacking shots, such as drives, cuts, and pulls, were really just a continuation of a forward and back defence. So, if you can't play the forward and back defensive shots correctly, then you may as well "take up darts" he said.

Another valuable lesson to me was that if the ball was delivered on the off side of the wicket, it MUST be hit to the off side. If the ball was bowled down the leg side, it MUST be hit to the leg side. If the ball was bowled directly in line with the stumps, play straight.

I use these rules today when I am invited to coach junior cricketers. If a junior can't grasp these simple concepts, then he/she will not progress. Perhaps then a dartboard may be an option. These rules also apply to adults.

Arch Grosvenor was a journalist with a career spanning 58 years in country and metropolitan newspapers. He wrote a book in 1983 titled *A long way from Tipperary – 58 Years of South Australian Journalism*. In that book there is a little story that really sums up my Dad. The extract reads as follows:

MAXIE

One of the most notorious of Australia's legendary practical jokers I have ever met was from the Waikerie district – Maxie. A woman visitor to the district remarked that she had never witnessed spotlight shooting. "Soon fix that," said Maxie as darkness fell. With the visitor in the passenger seat of his old buckboard, Maxie took the wheel with a loaded gun across his knees.

A fox was soon sighted. As the tempo of the outing mounted, Maxie roared his instructions clearly. "Take the spotlight. Keep it on him so we don't lose sight. Hold this for me too," he added thrusting something into the palm of the passenger's hand.

A shot rang out – the fox fell dead –the old buckboard

roared to a halt. As they got out of the vehicle, the visitor stood speechless at the swiftness of the whole event. Maxie then said, "Now you know how it is done, simple isn't it. Now you can give me back that thing in your hand." The passenger stood aghast, several deep impressions in the palm of her hand revealed that throughout the chase she had firmly clenched her fist into Maxie's false teeth."

He used to do the same to any unsuspecting umpire at the end that he was bowling from. Walking back to his bowling mark he'd call out to the umpire, "Here, hold this," and they would fall for it every time.

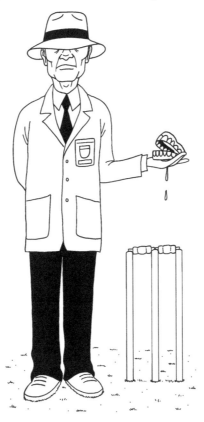

One set of his teeth went missing once when diving into the river. Legend has it that if you listen carefully, you can still hear the chattering. He did like a chat.

Arch also wrote that Dad was arguably the best country cricketer he had seen. In those days, working for a livelihood on the land prevented him, and other talented country cricketers, from shining on a bigger stage. Dad's brothers, Brook and Lindsay, were in the same situation, although Lindsay was a bit more fortunate. He played A-grade District Cricket for Woodville, played league football for Port Adelaide and ran in the Stawell Gift and the Bay Sheffield Athletics Carnival.

Dad, Brook and his sons, Wayne and Donn, along with Lindsay were all pivotal in shaping my career in one way or another. No other coaches or players throughout my career had said a word about, maybe, improving my batting, bowling or fielding. A real example of this was that I used to get out, more times than I would like to remember, being caught behind while leg glancing down the leg side or being bowled around my legs. This was the legacy of younger days playing in the school yard with no pads and trying to protect my legs. What would happen is that I would put my front foot too far to the off side causing me to over balance in that direction, instead of being more upright and more balanced. Even at first class level I pleaded with the so-called coaches for help. No help was forthcoming, and in reality, they were either too lazy or didn't have the expertise or both. Fellow players were also a bit reluctant to give advice, because in many cases, we were all vying for a place in a team. In fairness, and with hindsight, I should have taken some ownership and responsibility myself, but to depart from the 'coaching manual' was not the done thing. Perhaps a more open stance could have helped.

When I was younger, even a stint at a private boarding college, which boasted coaches of the highest order, was not too enlightening. In fact, the only thing I really remember about those coaches, or any of my junior coaches, was the authoritative way they would call out, telling you, that your batting time in the nets had finished. My time at college was full of mixed emotions and experiences. To sum it up its probably fair enough to say that I was just too immature. I did, however, enjoy the exeat weekends. Perhaps I had it too good at home.

Bob Gillies, a Primary School teacher at Ramco during the 1960s and 1970s instilled the importance of activities outside the classroom. This appealed to me no end. Bob, along with Dad, introduced junior sport to the school. It may have been only the odd game or coaching session here and there, yet it certainly gave me, and I'm sure others, the taste of competing and winning. Bob was not all that gifted in the sporting arena, but he would say jokingly, "Do as I ask, not as I do". He did, however, bowl a handy, if not loopy, off break.

Dad died in 1996 aged 73 years.

31. Good friends and great adventures

Two of the best

They say that laughter is the best tonic. In those times of poor form, sickness, injury or hardship, two of my teammates shone through like a beacon, and still do. Graeme Wood

Baz and I pretty much met for the first time on our way out to open the innings in our first Test together at Adelaide Oval. We hardly spoke a word. Three months later in the West Indies we were inseparable. Early in the tour we seemed to gravitate toward each other because of mutual interests apart from cricket and a shared sense of humour. I suppose these qualities are the hallmarks of any friendship, but when you have a person who can make you laugh at just about anything he soon becomes a good mate.

Baz has been mentioned many times in this collection of memories, and I could have written a hundred more stories about our friendship although it would probably embarrass us now in our more mature years.

We were a big part of each other's lives for only seven to eight years, but we can still pick up on a conversation where we left off – usually about something funny, or insignificant, or football. Then again, our conversations these days include a lot about family and grand kids. Who would have thought! One of my big regrets was being involved in his wedding and not being confident enough to give a speech. These days, I would have roasted him to a crisp.

Much has been written about us and being labelled the Kamikaze Kids because of our running between the wickets. There was never any blame, but afterwards we'd sit together quietly and feel each other's anguish.

I wish him well in retirement and to his lovely wife, Angela, and kids Brooke Christopher, Matthew, and Caitlin.

Sam Parkinson

Wow, what can I say without getting into too much trouble! Sam was fresh out of school, and I'm sure there was a sigh of relief in the staff room at Pembroke School when he joined his father, Dave, in the wholesale sporting goods business. I used to frequent the shop for gear, sometimes to scornful looks from Dave and generally have a chat with Sam. These pleasantries soon gave way to a more typical young men's talk.

Sam started playing State cricket with me and was immediately dubbed, by Hookesy, the shortest left arm fast bowler in the state. Hookesy was very apt at finding a chink in someone's amour. Sam laughed it off as he did most things. Not to be outdone he certainly returned the friendly insults – with interest!

Social events were plentiful, and it was a foregone conclusion that we would go together, and often be politely asked to leave.

Sam was best man at my wedding, while I was a groomsman at his. Marriage slowed us down a bit, but the fun times ran deep, and the silliness continued. He has always been there for me in good times or bad, and sometimes talking to a good friend is the only therapy one needs. Sam's generosity and loyalty know no bounds.

His humour is never ending. The short speech he gave at my 60th birthday party was a classic. He started with a joke, as he always did. It went sometime like this: "The Bell Ringer at St Peters Cathedral in Adelaide wanted to go on holidays, so he found himself a replacement. The new man was ringing away one Sunday morning when the bell swung back and hit him right in the face. The poor man fell out of the window and went splat on the street. The Bishop and a bystander rushed up to the man and the bystander asked the Bishop, 'Who is this man, what is his name?' The Bishop replied, **'I don't know his name but his face rings a bell".** The dead man's brother rushes up to the Bishop pleading, 'Mr Bishop, Mr Bishop you must give me the bell ringer's job in memory of my dead brother.' 'OK,' said the Bishop and before long the same thing happened, with the bell hitting the dead man's brother right on the head, causing him to fall out of the window and die on the street. The Bishop rushed out and a bystander said to the bishop, 'Mr Bishop, Mr Bishop who is this man, what is his name?' The bishop replied, **'I don't know his name, but he is a dead ringer for his brother.'**"

Famous newspaper columnist, Walter Winchell, once wrote: "A real friend walks in when the rest of the world walks out."

That sums up Sam Parkinson perfectly. I hope we have many more laughs together, but Sam has stipulated precedence is now given to his wife, Janet, and his kids Harry, Emily, Annabel and Alexandra, who is my god daughter.

32. A Special Mention

Nugget 60 years of support.

Most cricket purists associate the name 'Nugget' with the legendary Keith Miller. However, he was not a touring member of the South Australian and Australian sides for over a half a century, like Barry 'Nugget' Rees.

Nugget now 78, was anointed with this nickname (after his hero Keith Miller) by his employer Barry Jarman (BJ), Australian and South Australian wicket keeper, in 1962. Nugget, then 18, was grateful and proud as punch to become the errand boy for the famous Rowe and Jarman Sports Store in Grenfell Street, Adelaide.

Nugget soon became a familiar figure, walking the grey flagstones of the inner central business district delivering parcels and messages from the shop. BJ used to say that Nugget was an asset, as he was more reliable than Australia Post and more personal than the landline telephone. BJ soon invited Nugget to Adelaide Oval to watch the Sheffield Shield and Tests in which BJ was participating. That was the start of a fascinating cricket career for Nugget and was many a young boys' dream.

This likeable and very polite young man was soon asked to run errands to and from Adelaide Oval and the players became ever more reliant on Nugget to supply everything from jock straps and socks, to bats and boots from the store. Everything turned up on time, as Nugget was fastidious, and always reliable.

When I started in 1975, Nugget was well-entrenched and although BJ had retired from cricket, Nugget was still an integral part of the shop and the players' needs. By this time, he had his favourite seat in the players' viewing room. He had already been on tour with the South Australian team for many years and as a seasoned veteran the younger players treated him as a mentor, of sorts, and in doing so a unique bonding resulted.

Ian Chappell was captain then and Nugget was given the job of motivational speaker when we needed it. These talks were presented with him on top of the change room table, for maximum effect, and when the chairs were removed from around the table Nugget would have no way of getting down. He would laugh and laugh until someone helped him down. The content of the talks never changed much over the years I was there, but if you were doing good or going bad, either as a team, or as an individual, he would certainly let you know - in front of everyone.

The Inverarity and Hookes captaincy years followed,

as did the Lehmann and Siddons years and now Nugget has a brand-new seat in the viewing room, which came with the revamped improvements, next to the current captain, Travis Head. During Hookesy's time the rule of wearing batting gloves for Nugget was enforced on many occasions when his clapping got a little too zealous and sustained. This tradition is still alive and well.

His loyalty to the Australian and South Australian teams is unparalleled and has been for all this time. If he's not talking cricket he'll bring you up to date with the happenings of his beloved Port Adelaide Football Club, where he also has his own spot in their change rooms.

History has highlighted my association with Nugget from the Australian and South Australian teams to The Kensington District Cricket Club and The Port Adelaide Football Club. I worked only a short Russell Ebert stab pass from Nugget in the city and lived in the same suburb for a time. I used to drive him to the cricket, so we always had plenty to talk about. He now carries a walking stick but still has a sharp mind and wit and still looks like he did when I first met him.

It is a privilege for me to have been a part of his life for nearly half a century. I do wish, however, that I had been a little less grumpy when I had been given out and he was adamant that it was a no ball, too high, or didn't carry and so on.

Conclusion

ob Simpson's words to me, printed at the front of this book, ring even truer now than they did back in 1978. The catalyst for my greatest friendships has been sport, and cricket in particular. Some of those many friends appear in this book, and while others are not mentioned, they are no less in my memory. In my journey of over six decades, I like to think that I have a long list of friends. I hope some will include me in their own lists.

In the days when big bulky cameras were the norm for some, I however, chose to lock these memories away in my 'memory vault'. Some would say that there wasn't much going on in that vault anyway!

From junior football in Ramco through to the pinnacle of world cricket, sport has been good to me, and for me. I couldn't compete academically because of dyslexia, so my goal in life was to make dammed sure that I would compete hard and strive to achieve my best in sport.

When I was growing up, cricket and other mainstream sports, were not profitable vocations. These days, most are legitimate career paths. Coaches are an integral part of development, but cross sports, pursued in the school yard and back yards are much more important in honing your natural eye, footwork, athleticism, and flair. I was fortunate that my backyard was as big as I wanted it to be.

It will soon be identified which sport and discipline you are most suited to. That may be true, but if you are not enjoying or getting fun out of the game, or in other words if the bad times outweigh the good times, don't be afraid to change.

The writing this book was conceived while whiling away the idle hours on jury duty. It started as a nothing more than a doodle on some scrap paper, which turned into a letter, then a word, then a sentence and so on, and the memories were ignited. It was put on hold for some time, due to a heart attack, which was followed by an emergency quadruple bypass in March 2021.

Fortunately, I am still on the right side of the soil . It rammed home the importance of a loving family, good friends, and unforgettable experiences!